GROWING UP IN
Little Egypt

Enjoy this book
about my wonderful
dad. Happy Reading
Linda

GROWING UP IN
Little Egypt

THE REST OF THE STORY

LINDA LEE REAM

iUniverse, Inc.
Bloomington

Growing Up in Little Egypt
The Rest of the Story

iUniverse books may be ordered through booksellers or by contacting:

iUniverse
1663 Liberty Drive
Bloomington, IN 47403
www.iuniverse.com
1-800-Authors (1-800-288-4677)

ISBN: 978-1-4759-0173-3 (sc)
ISBN: 978-1-4759-0174-0 (ebk)

Library of Congress Control Number: 2012905236

Printed in the United States of America

iUniverse rev. date: 04/14/2012

CONTENTS

Growing Up in Little Egypt
By Eldon Lee
As told to Linda Lee Ream in 2009-10

Part 3

Part 4

Part 5

As We Sat
By Linda Lee Ream
The Rest of the Story
By Linda Lee Ream

To the memory of my parents,
Eldon M. and Isabel McAlpin Lee

Introduction

By Linda Lee Ream

I want to tell you about my wonderful father, Eldon Lee. Dad lived for ninety-six years, and in this book you will learn about his family, the place in southern Illinois where he grew up, and how he was molded by the many changes that occurred during his long lifetime: World War One, the Roaring Twenties, the Depression, and World War Two, to name a few. In his last year on earth, we sat together for many hours while he told me precious tales about the first third of his life. I look forward to sharing them with you.

Dad was born deep in the southern part of Illinois. Far from Chicago's skyscrapers and central Illinois' prairies, the pointy end of Illinois resembles an arrowhead. As it narrows to a tip, the distance between the two mighty rivers dwindles from eighty to forty to twenty miles until, at Cairo, you see the Ohio meet the Mississippi. Locals call this the "land between the rivers" or "Little Egypt," because of its resemblance to the Nile River. Another theory is that the Egypt reference originated when northern Illinois settlers came south to buy grain during the poor harvest of the 1830s, similar to the Book of Genesis's account of ancient people traveling to Egypt for grain.

A traveler driving south from Chicago encounters scenery consisting mostly of flat, sprawling crop lands. It would be extremely easy to assume the entire state of Illinois consists of such a landscape; however, as you continue south, crop lands gradually fade and the tableau becomes multidimensional. You begin to see trees, wild vegetation, lakes, and cliffs.

Deep Roots in Southern Illinois

Many of the settlers of southern Illinois were descendents of people from Scotland and Ireland who had come to this country before 1776 and lived in the hill regions of Kentucky, Tennessee, the Carolinas, and Virginia before moving to Little Egypt. The history of both sides of our family reflects this.

The paternal branch of the family came to Illinois from Virginia, and it is said by some family members that the first Lee, Robert Lee, who migrated to southern Illinois in 1835, was a cousin of the famous Confederate general, Robert E. Lee. The maternal side of Dad's family first came to Little Egypt in 1816 after residing in Greensboro, North Carolina; Ohio; and Indiana.

GROWING UP IN LITTLE EGYPT

By Eldon Lee
As told to Linda Lee Ream in 2009-10

PART 1

MY FAMILY

My father's parents were Rev. Robert William Lee, a Baptist minister, and Josephine Phillips Lee. They had nine children: Marion (my father), John, Norman, Bird, Effie Lee Perry, Elsie Lee Smith, Inman (also a well-known Baptist minister), Mallie, and Cordah Lee Phillips. Several of these uncles and aunts lived on farms near where I was born and lived my first six years. For the most part, this was the side of the family that set a good example for me in my youth.

Grandpa Rev. Robert W. Lee

The parents of my mother, Cora Minton Lee, were Ella Jones Minton and Henry Minton. Their children were Cora, Guy, Ray, Carrie, Roy, Carroll, Omar, and Ita Minton Newman. Grandpa Henry Minton was someone I never wanted to copy. He would leave his wife and children and take off for days in his horse and buggy. He told us that he wanted to find a rich woman with a farm. In his later years, after his wife had died, he accomplished this goal.

Grandpa Henry Minton

My mother's brothers had two things in common. First, they owned small businesses: two owned restaurants, two had butcher shops, another ran a grocery store, and one operated an appliance store. Unfortunately, most of them also shared a severe drinking problem. I believe both of these factors influenced my adult life in positive ways. I followed their drive to be self-employed and ended up owning my own lumberyard. On the other hand, because their excessive drunkenness was a negative influence in my young life, I have always been careful about my intake of alcohol.

THE BEGINNING
OF MY JOURNEY

(1913-27)

I was born September 27, 1913, the last of nine children. As was common in those days, three of my siblings—Chalon, Emerson, and Hallie—had died in infancy. The other children born before me were Minnie (1897), Rosa (1901), Elvah (1903), Paul (1908), and Lura (1910). Elvah passed away in 1921 from pneumonia when she was eighteen. At that time, she and Rosa were living and working at a mental institution upstate in Kankakee.

I was given the unusual name of Eldon because when my mother was pregnant with me, she met a man by that name. As the family story goes, he was helping build a bridge over Reed Ford Creek, which was near the house where I was born. I have no idea where my middle name, Maurice (they pronounced it Morris), came from. I seriously doubt that they knew it was a French name. I always wished I had a simple name, such as Bob, Bill, or Jim. In my business life, many people just called me Lee.

Earliest Memories

(1916-19)

I was born on a small farm about a mile and a half from Akin, Illinois. Akin is a very tiny town of approximately 150 souls in southern Illinois. I lived there until I was six or seven. We grew corn, wheat, oats, and something called stock peas, which we fed to the cattle. We also had a vegetable garden. After our family ate the produce, pigs, and cattle, we had a very minimal amount left to sell. I do remember taking eggs and cream and selling them at the store. The farm families helped each other with baling hay, threshing wheat, and raising barns. Hog-killing day was a big day for me and all the other little kids. My favorite part was when the men put a knife in the pig and the blood spurted out all over the place. Also, the fresh sausage and liver were delicious treats I looked forward to eating soon after the hog was killed and dressed. Everything on our farm was done without any type of help from machinery. As a little kid, I had fun following my dad to the barn to help him feed the horses, cows, and chickens. When we had big snowstorms, I had to step into my dad's footprints to make it to the barn.

My Parents, Cora and Marion Lee

On our farm, we had a large mutt named Jack. Jack loved to go rabbit hunting. When he would bring home a prized rabbit, my mother would cook it and serve it with biscuits and gravy. Nothing has ever tasted better than those rabbits that Jack caught!

There was a small Baptist church very close to our house. I liked to go there on Sundays to see the many horses and buggies parked around the church. Although my Grandpa Lee was getting old, he still preached there occasionally in exchange for a ham or any money that they might collect.

I remember when I was three or four, I ran barefoot through white ashes that were still hot from an outdoor fire. We usually only wore our shoes on Sunday or when there was snow on the ground, so I ran around with bare feet most of the time. When I unknowingly walked through the ashes, my feet were severely burned and hurt so much that I can still remember the pain over ninety years later. The only treatment was for me was to stay off them until they healed. This seemed like a very long time to a young boy.

At about four, I went on a hike in the woods with four or five boys, including my big brother, Paul, who was about nine at the time. One of the older boys killed a rabbit with a shotgun. We built a fire and roasted and ate the rabbit. I still recall how great that food tasted!

At the tender age of three and four, I was free to roam from farm to farm. I liked to visit my Grandpa and Grandma Lee, who lived on a farm about one-half mile from my house. I also loved to walk the one-half mile in the other direction to visit Uncle John's farm and play with my thirteen cousins of all ages. Uncle John's wife, Aunt Vinnie, made good "hard bread" that all of the children loved to eat. My sister, Lura, and I visited the Akin area in 2007 and found Uncle John's house still standing. Aunt Elsie, Uncle Jesse, and Uncle Doug Phillips also had farms nearby.

I also remember receiving an orange or banana for a Christmas present. What a rare treat that was! Mostly, Christmas was a time when we went to church more often. I can't recall ever having a birthday party or getting any presents for that occasion.

When I was about four, I went skinny dipping with other boys from the neighborhood. Our favorite place was nearby Reed Ford Creek, which had a small sandy beach. I particularly remember the time a boy who had been circumcised was visiting the area. We all laughed and kidded him because we thought his penis had been cut off.

I still recall a time when my dad was going to town and he told me I couldn't go. I hid on a board, called the coupling, in the back of his wagon. Dad stopped to talk to a neighbor, who saw my feet and said, "Marion, whose feet are those sticking out of your wagon?" Instead of being punished, I got to sit up on the seat next to my dad. When we got to the store, I saw, for the first time in my life, a boy with an ice cream cone. I really wanted one, so my dad gave me a nickel. When I went into the store by myself, I was too shy to say anything to the clerk. A kind customer asked me if I wanted an ice cream cone and bought one for me.

My first educational experience was at Fizzle Ridge, a one-room school near my house. There were children up to eighth grade attending this school, but I only went there for one year. My main memory is of having an urgent need to go to the outhouse but being too shy to ask permission of the teacher. When I finally got up enough nerve to ask, I ran as fast as I could because I thought all of the kids in the school were watching me as I hurried to make it in time.

In 1918, everyone in our household, except me, caught the dangerous Spanish flu that was sweeping the world. Since everyone was too sick to do any work and I was too young, my family had a man come in to help us. He brought some whiskey, which was supposed to cure the flu. I remember trying a little drink and finding it far too bitter. I didn't like it at all! We even had a doctor come to see the patients. I spent most of my time hanging out in the yard and watching anyone who came by. Fortunately, the family all recovered.

In 1919, we had a complete crop failure because there was no rain and bugs ate the crops. My parents made the decision to sell the farm and move to town, where my dad was able to get a job at a coal mine. We moved all of our household goods by horse and wagon about twenty miles from Akin, to the much larger town of West Frankfort.

GROWING UP IN
WEST FRANKFORT

(1920-27)

This was a tough move for me. I went from a one-room school to Logan School, which was in a great big three-story building. Evidently, they didn't think very much of my year at Fizzle Ridge since they put me in first grade again. The kids at my new school made fun of me because I came from a farm. When these bullies chased me home, my mother said, "Eldon just go back outside and fight them." I didn't fight at that time, but I later made friends who helped me with the bullies. A boy who lived down the street soon became my best friend. His name was Randolph "Randy" Peak, and we were good buddies for a long time. When Randy and I were about thirty, we were drafted to serve in World War II. Unfortunately for Randy, we took different paths in the navy. After boot camp at Great Lakes, I went to Oklahoma for further training, and Randy was assigned to a destroyer in the Pacific. He lost his life in the Battle of the Philippines in 1944.

At that time, West Frankfort was a town of about eighteen thousand people. We moved to the hilly section called Frankfort Heights. This part of town had its own small business district that was about a block and a half long.

There was a barber shop, movie theater, car repair garage, grocery store, confectionery, feed store, doughnut factory, and hardware store. The main downtown later developed on the flat part of town when the railroad ran through there. We bought a house at 1703 East Poplar Street. This house seemed large to me at the time. It had five rooms, including a large living room, dining room, and kitchen. There was a large bedroom where my parents slept, and a small one for Paul, Lura, and me. As I recall, we were the only three children left at home then. I vividly remember when Grandpa Minton came to our house. He always slept with me and yelled and complained about the way I moved around all night. I dreaded his visits. This house had big porches on the front and the back. My workshop area was under the back porch. This was where I put together my little wagons and cars.

In the back of this house there was a large garden (about seventy-five yards long and forty-five feet wide) where we grew vegetables, such as lettuce, onions, potatoes, sweet corn, and tomatoes. Dad hired someone with a team of horses to plow the ground before he did the planting. I helped Dad with the hoeing, although I didn't like to do it. There was also a small barn and an outhouse in back of our house. Our 1919 Model T Ford was parked in a little lean-to that was built on the barn.

My Grown Sisters: (left to right) Elvah, Minnie, and Rosa

The outdoor toilet played a greater role in my youth than I would have preferred. When I was naughty, my folks would threaten to lock me in the outhouse at night. They told me a story about an old lady called Black Annie who went around the neighborhood at night beating up on people and robbing them. I don't remember ever being locked up, but the threats did scare me. At that time, I had seen only one person with black skin, a peddler who came into town during the day to sell his corn. All the kids followed him around because he looked different. The story goes that black people were told that they must be out of town at sunset. I never heard how the alleged rule was enforced, but there were no blacks living in West Frankfort. At that time, I didn't ask questions about it. I definitely didn't want to run into Black Annie when she was wandering around at night.

During that period, I heard a radio for the first time. It was small and looked like a cigar box. Some people even made their own radios by buying the crystals and putting them in cigar boxes. Majestic and Philco were the main manufacturers of the first radios. One of our neighbors bought one, and we were all happy when they invited us over to listen. We didn't have a local station so we tried faraway stations. We got the best reception from KDKA in Pittsburgh, which was three states away. We also sometimes received WLW in Cincinnati, KSD in St. Louis, and WLS in Chicago. Some of my favorite shows were *The Grand Ole Opry*, *Fibber McGee and Molly*, and *Lum and Abner*. The reception was usually spotty from all the stations, and when it stormed, all we could hear was static. After a while, a Philco that sat on the table and had a rounded top began to get better reception.

At our house, we had an Edison wind-up phonograph machine that played flat disc 78 rpm records.

Having a Good Time

I found many ways to have fun after we moved to West Frankfort. For example, I loved to play baseball with the neighborhood boys in a nearby field. Another fun activity was building little wagons in my workshop under the porch. I would try to find four wheels, lumber, and an old buggy wheel in some scrap pile. I begged my mother for nickels so I could buy nails at the hardware store. After I put these little vehicles together, I would ride them down the hill near our house. What fun!

I enjoyed being a Boy Scout at Logan School. I recall the troop building a fire and cooking baked potatoes. We covered them with mud and threw them in the fire. When they were done, we removed the mud and had a real treat. I also tried to get merit badges by doing good deeds, such as helping an old lady across the street. I still remember the Boy Scout motto: "Do a good deed daily and always be prepared."

Our house was about a block from a doughnut factory on Main Street. They made delicious glazed doughnuts, which sold for a nickel apiece. Sometimes I'd buy one with the money I was supposed to be taking for the collection at Sunday school. This was a risk because my dad was my Sunday school teacher. To this day, I don't know if he realized that I didn't drop anything into the collection plate when it was passed. If he noticed, he didn't say anything to me.

I started having an interest in girls at an early age. When I was about seven or eight, I had my first sweetheart, Thelma Lawrence. She lived about three or four blocks from me. In those days, we just "claimed" sweethearts. I liked her, but didn't know how she felt about me. I also played with Claude Hayes and his sister. Their family had a small barn and we would get up in the loft and try to do naughty things. Today our activities would probably seem acceptable because we didn't remove any clothing. My girlfriend in the third or fourth grade was Edith Baer. Forty years later, I ran into her at a party at a friend's house in Springfield. I was interested in a girl named Ruby in about fourth or fifth grade. I was a little unruly while I was courting her in the classroom, and my teacher took me outside and said, "You think you can get away with everything because your dad is on the school board." This was a surprise to me since no one had told me that Dad was on the board.

Eldon in his Early Teens

Every year when I was in grade school, I spent a week in the summertime with my sister, Rosie, and her husband, Frank Corn, on their farm. My sister had been married as long as I could remember, and I liked her husband even though he often thought of ways to tease me. One story I remember well was when Uncle Frank finally let me ride his bull, Till Bill. In those days, I wanted to be a cowboy and constantly begged him to let me ride the bull. One day Uncle Frank tied the bull to a fence so I could get on him. Then he untied the bull and slapped him on the back with a rope, and I went off his back into corncobs, manure, and mud. I was such a mess when I got up that I completely lost my desire to be a cowboy.

Eldon in Seventh Grade at Logan School
(second from left in the first row)

THE TRISTATE TORNADO

On March 18, 1925, when I was eleven years old, I stayed home from school because I wasn't feeling well. It was just my mother and me in the house that day. It started raining very hard and got extremely dark outside. We had no warning that the worst tornado in history was approaching from the west. Mother was wringing her hands and pacing the floor. We heard the big wind come and later learned that we were a few blocks away from the eye of the storm. Our house was spared, but when I went outside, I saw many houses in my neighborhood burning from fires caused by overturned coal stoves. I started walking around town and saw bodies all over the place and lines of cars coming to take the wounded to the hospital. These scenes made a lasting impression on me, and I can still see them vividly eighty-four years later.

This terrible tornado that I had experienced was the Great Tristate Tornado of March 18, 1925, that at 1:01 in the afternoon had started its uninterrupted 219 mile trek from its origin in the Missouri Ozarks. The tornado tore across Missouri and southern Illinois, and finally lifted three and one-half hours later in southwestern Indiana. The mass of violent blackness killed 695 people, injured 2027 people, destroyed 15,000 homes, and damaged 164 square miles (almost 50 times the average tornado). Twenty percent of West Frankfort was destroyed.

Early Car Experiences

We bought a Model T Ford after we moved to West Frankfort and Dad started making some money working at the mine. Uncle John was still living on the farm and also bought a Model T. It was impossible for him to get all thirteen of his kids in the car. When he came to visit once, he said, "I just threw a few of the little kids in the car and came to see you." These were the days long before seat belts, air bags, and any kind of child restraints. One time when we were in church, our Model T was stolen even though Dad had the keys in his hand. We later found the car and it had been completely stripped. The tires, battery, and everything that could be sold were gone. We just had a skeleton of a Model T. I vaguely remember that they bought parts and put it back together. They never caught the thief.

My father was never a very good driver. He always acted as if he were driving a team of horses. We laughed when he said, "Whoa," at the same time that he put on the brakes. I first drove when a man at the repair garage asked me if I could drive. I said yes even though I had never driven in my life. He wanted me to drive four or five miles out to the country with him, to a farm, to pick up a cow he had purchased. My job was to follow him with the car while he walked the cow back to town. I had to stop every so often for him to catch up with me. I had to crank the car to get it started again every time I stopped. The garage owner thought I had done an okay job of driving. This was before a license was required to drive a vehicle.

We occasionally took road trips to visit my mom's only sister, Ita. She lived about ninety miles from us in Cynthana, Indiana, on a large dairy farm with her family of seven or eight kids and a husband. At first we made the trip in our 1919 Ford that had many flat tires and an engine that would boil over when it got too hot. We did all the work that was needed to keep the car going. We patched our own tires with a product called Camel Tire Patch, and we fixed the engine when it quit operating. Our first trip took almost all day. We took fried chicken for a picnic lunch and arrived in Indiana in the late afternoon. Our next car was a 1925 Model T Ford that had balloon tires, which gave us a better ride than the hard, high tires of our previous car. It also had an injection system that I think was all electric. With that car, we got to Aunt Ita's before lunch and still had our fried chicken.

Another car I remember was a 1927 Chevrolet. I once drove it with several of my friends along and accidentally let the radiator run out of water. When I realized what I had done, I made another mistake and put cold water in the radiator. This caused the valves to warp. I was afraid that Dad wouldn't let me drive the Chevy anymore, but I don't think he said much about it and just went and had it repaired.

The roads near my house were all dirt, so if it rained too much, it was difficult to get home in the mud. A few main roads were covered with gravel, and to keep them smooth, horses would pull a log or some kind of wooden platform over them. My father was a road commissioner during this time.

First Moneymaking Jobs

When I was about twelve, I asked my barber if I could shine shoes at the empty shoeshine chair in his shop. I bought my own supplies: a special liquid to wipe the mud off shoes and shoe paste. My shoeshine technique was as follows: first, I removed all the mud with a liquid; then I applied a coat of paste and brushed the shoes; and finally, I applied a second coat of paste and made the shoes really shine using a rag. After I was finished, I whipped the rag and made it pop. All of this cost the customer a dime. I averaged three or four dollars on Saturday and the same amount on Sunday. Although the barber shop wasn't open on Sunday, the owner let me open up so I could do my business. At that time in West Frankfort, the Ku Klux Klan would march through town in their white robes and hats. I was able to identify many of the marchers because I recognized their nicely shined shoes. With the money I was making, I bought doughnuts and ice cream for myself and sometimes helped my family out with groceries.

This would be a good time to explain more about the KKK in southern Illinois in the twenties. Their central rallying cry was prohibition of alcohol. In nearby "Bloody Williamson" County, the KKK was very actively fighting against the open bootlegging that was happening there.

West Frankfort, in Franklin County, didn't seem to have as many open violations of the prohibition of alcohol, but the KKK was ready for whatever might happen. My father believed that the Klan did good things, but he never told us whether he was a member or what the good things were. We suspected that he probably belonged.

I also worked at the Family Theatre, which was across the street from the barber shop where I shined shoes. I pumped the player piano that served as the background music for the silent movies. I sometimes had to change the rolls for the piano. My pay for pumping was the ability to watch the movies. I got to see movies featuring Tom Mix and his horse, Rex; Hoot Gibson; and *Around the World in Eighty Days* with Eddie Polo. The owner of the theater was named A. Blenkin, which we thought sounded like Abe Lincoln.

Another activity I enjoyed during this period was modeling men's clothing for J. V. Walker, the leading men's clothing store. Every year when the local Majestic Theatre had a fashion show for the ladies who were attending a cooking school, I was called upon to model. This job didn't pay anything but was somewhat prestigious in our town.

A Handsome Model

Family Life and Influences

I will forever remember that my dad was a good man. A quiet man, he lived his religion rather than talked about it. He taught Sunday school every Sunday at the Second Baptist Church in Frankfort Heights. As I mentioned, Dad was on the school board and, I later learned, he also served on the city council. During this period, he worked at the coal mine. He was usually assigned to work on top of the mine, organizing the coal cars. In the summers when coal wasn't being used as much, his hours would drop to one or two days a week and his pay would be significantly cut. Dad chewed tobacco constantly (he never smoked cigarettes) and, as a result, when he was older, his teeth were halfway worn off. I don't believe he ever went to a dentist.

I was expected to attend both Sunday school and church in those days. Our church was Southern Baptist, and the first preacher I remember was Rev. Lowry, who gave half-day fire-and-brimstone sermons and told us we couldn't go to movies or dances. I went to sleep while he ranted about evil. I did believe the stories that we were taught and remember being scared of going to hell. I also remember a minister named Paul Smith, who was better-educated and had quieter sermons. The problem with him was that he used big words that the congregation couldn't understand. At that time, there was a split in the church, and about half of the congregation left and started a church of their own, named Calvary Baptist.

Many times after church, we would go to Sunday dinner with one of the families from the church. This was when I really would get bored. Sometimes I would be allowed to leave these dinners and walk up to two miles home. Although we always attended church, my parents didn't talk about religion at home and we didn't give thanks before meals.

My parents belonged to several organizations, both in the church and in the community. Mother belonged to Ladies Aid at church, an organization that helped less fortunate folks. My dad was a member of the Odd Fellows, and Mother belonged to the Rebekahs, the ladies' group associated with the Odd Fellows. Mom also was a member of the Royal Neighbors. These community organizations were fraternal and shared a belief in a supreme being. The Royal Neighbors group was started in Iowa with the purpose of making life insurance available for women. They are all still active today.

Sometimes the Odd Fellows and the Rebekahs would have meetings together in their lodge, which was over the Stotlar-Herrin Lumber Company in the Frankfort Heights. When they took me with them, I was really bored by their ceremonies, which included waltzing around the room. I didn't have any idea what any of their rituals meant.

My Mother at a Rebekahs Meeting

I recall that my mom was much more talkative than my dad. She was outgoing and social at home, in the church, and in the community. She was also extremely busy running a household without modern conveniences. Sewing clothes for the family with a Singer sewing machine that she had to peddle was a big job for her. I wore shirts that she had made for me.

We had three big meals a day that she prepared. For breakfast, we had biscuits, bacon, and fried eggs. The noon meal was called dinner and consisted of vegetables from our garden, mashed potatoes, some kind of meat—pork, beef, or veal—and corn bread or homemade rolls or bread. Supper was the evening meal, and we ate pretty much the same type of things we had at dinner. Chicken was reserved for Sunday dinner. All of these meals were cooked on a kerosene stove. We used coal oil that I was sent to purchase at the store for ten cents a gallon. A gallon would last us for about week. This product had little odor and produced a blue flame that looked like gas. At that time, we used coal in our heat stove. My married sister, Rosie, lived on a farm with lots of woods, so she used wood for fuel in a type of stove called a cook stove.

During that period, fried chicken was my favorite food. One time I picked up a corncob and hit a three-pound rooster on the head and broke his neck. I finished killing it by pulling its head off. We had to eat the chicken that day because we had no way to keep it cool. My mother yelled at me when she had to break the rule of chicken only on Sundays. At that time, the only way we could keep something fresh was by hanging it in the well, where it was cooler.

A few other impressions related to food have stayed with me through the years. I liked the dumplings my mother made. These dumplings were rolled out and cut in strips and looked like a thick noodle. She boiled them with chicken and sometimes with peas or other vegetables that she picked fresh from the garden.

My dad ate everything using just a knife. We were all amazed when he could balance peas on his knife. When he went to work at the mine, he carried a coal miner's lunch bucket. The bucket was made of tin; in the bottom of the bucket was water for lunch, the top of the upper section of the bucket was a compartment for a couple of sandwiches or some fruit, and then there was the lid.

My Brother

Paul was five years older than me. While we were living in the Frankfort Heights, he worked at the Coalfield store on the main street in the business district of West Frankfort. Coalfield's sold general merchandise to miners using a form of payment called scrip. The miners could use scrip like real money and it would be taken out of their next paycheck at the coal mine. The prices were higher because of this convenience. Coalfield's delivered groceries in a wagon pulled by two horses and sometimes the driver would let me ride with him on his route.

When Paul was about seventeen and working at the store, an unknown affliction gradually began to cause him to drag his feet, pitch forward, and trot. His mind was not affected at all, and he was not confined to his bed. Our parents took him to doctors all over southern Illinois, St. Louis, and Chicago, looking for a diagnosis. I never figured out where they got the money to pay for these trips and for the doctors. Although there was never a definite diagnosis, it was sometimes called sleeping sickness. In the midtwenties, there was an epidemic of a disease by that name that attacked younger people. Before he lost his coordination, he had been a good basketball player.

Paul (left) Playing Basketball with a Friend

In 1927, Dad decided to return to farming, which had always been his first love. At that time, the mines were beginning to shut down because they were running out of coal, and he wasn't making a good living anymore.

BACK TO FARM LIFE

PART 2

(1927-33)

LIVING IN A
CHICKEN HOUSE

My folks traded their house in the Frankfort Heights for an eighty-acre farm about a mile and a half away. The only structure on the farm was a barn. Dad decided to build a large chicken house that we could live in temporarily until he could get enough money together to build our real house.

I still remember how the chicken house was constructed. The floor consisted of boards placed on concrete blocks to hold it up. The 1 x 8 inch wide shiplap lapped over on the edges so there were no cracks. The framing material was 2 x 4 studs placed about four feet on centers. The exterior walls were built using 1 x 8 inch wide shiplap. The roof sheeting was made out of the same lumber. The cheapest lumber was used for everything in the chicken house. There was no dry wall and the studs were exposed. The size of the entire chicken house was 576 square feet. It was divided into three small rooms: a bedroom where Paul and I slept, a kitchen, and a living room. There was a little lean-to off the kitchen, where my parents slept. Dad also built a porch across the front of the house. A tar-paper roof on the house leaked every time it rained. I remember being a little ashamed to be living in a chicken house. My sister, Lura, was mostly out of the house when we lived there, but when she was ninety-seven she still didn't want to talk about that experience with me. We never built a regular house on the farm. I lived in the chicken house on and off for four or five years.

We had no electricity or any other modern convenience. Our main entertainment was listening to a battery-operated radio. We had a stove that used kerosene oil. It was extremely hot in the summer in the chicken house, and, of course, we had no fans or air-conditioning. Our well was our only source of drinking water. One day, someone found a snake in the well and Dad got it out. To this day, I can't figure out how he removed the snake.

When we first moved to the farm, I liked it because I could ride our two horses, Dick and Barney, on the weekends. I don't believe I rode horses again until I was eighty-five and visited my grandson in Colorado and enjoyed riding a horse named Hawk.

After a while, I started not liking farm life because there was so little money. After we moved to the farm, my parents didn't have any extra to give me, so from then on I had to earn my own way.

WORK, WORK, WORK ON THE FARM

Dad and I worked from six to six on the farm. By that time, Paul's affliction kept him from helping. Our many tasks included pitching the hay in the wagon and then pitching it into the barn loft. Dad and I killed and dressed a pig. I also fed the chickens, gathered the eggs, and milked the cows.

In our very large garden, we raised hay, stock peas for the stock, field and sweet corn, sweet potatoes, Irish potatoes, Kentucky Wonder green beans that we put next to the corn so they grew up on the corn stalks, lettuce, carrots, rhubarb, butter beans, parsnips, cabbage, peas for table eating, onions, and tomatoes. We used the horses for plowing, and Dad and I chopped the weeds out of the garden and hoed it regularly.

Our farm had an area with white oak trees that we would chop down in the winter and cut into fence posts. We would then take them to town, where they sold for twenty-five cents each to people who had preordered them.

I also had some extra farm-related jobs. One day, Dad asked me to take a cow in heat over to a neighbor to get her bred. I completed the task, brought the cow back home, and eleven months later, we had a calf. We weren't even charged a fee for this service. I also helped a neighbor farmer, Mr. Miller, bale hay. I put many one-hundred-pound square hay bales in the barn for him, and he paid my dad instead of me. This was very disappointing to me, but I realized that the money was needed to buy groceries for our family. We had to purchase items, such as sugar, flour, lard, and coal oil. Sometimes we were able to sell eggs to the grocer to help pay for what we needed to buy.

The most unpleasant job I was asked to do on the farm was to deal with a bad dog that came on our farm and killed chickens and broke eggs. Mom told me to put a rope around the dog's neck and take it to the creek that ran through the wooded area in the back of our property. She gave me an old gun and told me to shoot it, and I did.

Somehow I always knew that my dad liked farming more than my mother did. We could figure out when our parents were having a spat even though they didn't fight in front of us. The biggest clue was when Dad slept all night on the hay in the barn.

EIGHTH-GRADE SCHOOL EXPERIENCES

When we moved to the country, I had to change schools. I started eighth grade at Snipe Flat School, a two-room school with no indoor plumbing. Of course, there were no school buses and I had to walk a mile and a half twice a day. I walked with my neighbors, Faye and Milton Taylor. Lura would later marry their older brother, Carl Taylor. Another interesting tidbit is that at my mother's ninety-ninth birthday celebration, Faye told me that she had been in love with me during the time we were walking together. I asked her why she waited such a very long time to tell me.

The two teachers at the school were Mr. Meyers and his daughter, Bernice, who was my teacher. I clearly remember the day that she sent me home for misbehaving. I got in a fight with Off Miller, the son of the man I had helped bale hay. I believe the fight occurred because Off was making fun of my brother's condition. After I walked the one and a half miles home, my dad told me to get in the car, and he took me right back to school. Now that was punishment!

I attended Snipe Flat School for one year and then took the examination for my graduation certificate. Our eighth-grade class went to Central High in West Frankfort to take the test, and they told us if we had passed. A small graduation ceremony was then held. As it turned out, that was to be my last school graduation until many years later when I completed a training course in the navy.

High School Years

I went to the only high school in West Frankfort, Frankfort Community High School, for approximately four years. The school was about two miles from the farm, and I had to use foot power to get there since no buses or other rides were available.

According to an old report card of mine, I made average grades. My favorite subject was called Manual Training. In that class, I built a small table out of oak and a matching magazine rack. My folks thought they were both nice and used them in their homes for the remainder of their lives. I also liked the part of the same class called mechanical drawing. That skill came in handy when I later had a long career in the lumber business. I didn't like English classes and dropped my French class after trying it for a while.

I thought sports were more fun than studying for classes. I went out for football, but I was too short and too light to make the team. Although the assistant coach was my cousin, I didn't get a chance to run with the ball since I was put in the line, which wasn't a good fit for my body type. I played some baseball on the playground because it wasn't sponsored by our school. My favorite sport was basketball, but I was never able to make the high school team. So I played in a big barn called Dimmick's Barn near Logan School, which had a basketball hoop at each end of the barn. I also played in a church league. I switched to the Christian church so I could play forward on their team.

When I was a freshman in high school and played basketball after school in the big barn, I had to walk the two miles home in the dark. I ran all the way home and took a shortcut through an abandoned coal mine. It was very creepy. Next, I ran between the barn and a house on a farm. I was afraid of the dog on this farm. Then I had to climb over a high fence that I had difficulty finding in the dark and was afraid that I might run into when I was running fast. I endured all of this rather than take the route along the road, which would have taken longer.

DANCING TO THE BIG BANDS

During my sophomore and junior high school years, I started going to dances. At this time there were no school-sponsored parties, so we found our fun at dance halls, such as the Hangar in Marion (a town about twelve miles away). This was a converted old airplane hangar that attracted big bands. Another dance venue in Marion was Costolanos, where I remember seeing Ben Bernie, a famous leader of a band, who was known for always having a cigar in his mouth. White City Park in the neighboring town of Herrin was another dance hall I frequented. We paid about one dollar to get into these places for the evening. We took our own liquor. During that time, we didn't experiment with drugs, but we did see the band members openly dip their cigarettes in cocaine and smoke them. Only the musicians did this.

Although I didn't have a car, I could always get a ride with a bunch of other boys and girls. We would all meet on Saturday night at a downtown drug store. My lifelong friend, Burt Jordan, always had a car because he worked part-time for the Ford Agency. Another friend was Louie Boner, whose dad owned a milk company, and if there was no other transportation available, we would go to the dance in his milk truck, an old Hupmobile.

I have to say, in looking back, I was in the popular group and never had any trouble getting a girlfriend. Doyle Roberts was a very pretty girl from Marion who I met at the dances. She was not very bright and ended up causing me to have one of my few fights. Her former boyfriend said that he would beat up anyone he caught with Doyle. One night we did go outside for a fight, and somehow I managed to get the first lick in his jaw because the old boyfriend wasn't quite ready to fight yet. That was the end of that ordeal.

A popular and pretty girlfriend from West Frankfort was Eva Epperheimer. She went with someone who had a Dodge before we started dating. Also, during this time, I met a girl, Margaret, from Ziegler, which was a town six miles away. She sold tickets at the local movie theater. I hitchhiked there many times because I liked her and thought she was smart. In 1933, she moved to Los Angeles and I moved to Chicago. She wanted me to visit her in Los Angeles, but I could never get the money together for the trip

Sometime during this period, I met Isabel McAlpin at a dance. We were both dating and dancing with other people, but in a few years we would get married and say it was because we enjoyed dancing together. We broke the dance hall's rule of no kissing while dancing. This marriage lasted almost seventy-two years.

STAYING AT UNCLE OMAR'S HOUSE

During my high school years, I sometimes lived with Uncle Omar (my mother's brother) and his family in West Frankfort. I did this for two reasons: he lived very close to the high school, and I had the opportunity to work for Uncle Omar in the butcher shop he managed in the Woodway Grocery Store. Although Uncle Omar had his faults, he was a fun-loving guy and the customers all seemed to like him. Alcohol was his problem. On Saturdays, he would buy four to eight gallons of whiskey and put it on the sawdust that was covering the blocks of ice in the walk-in cooler. He attached a hose to the whiskey barrel so he could take swigs of whiskey all day. By six in the evening, he was tired and went home, leaving me to clean up the place. My other job was to grind beef for hamburgers. On the weekends, we would have specials for ten cents a pound. I would grind everything I could find—cheese, pork, very fatty beef—in a large washtub.

I got free room and board at Uncle Omar's house. His wife, Bernice, didn't like the arrangement and many times made me feel unwanted. I figured this was probably because she had three younger children and was very busy. I remember she was constantly browbeating Omar, but when he got drunk, I saw him hit her.

Once when I was working at the Woodway store, I was out on the street during my break, talking with my dad. We saw a man who was being chased run all the way through the store and out the back door, where he was shot by his pursuer on the porch of the funeral home that was directly in back of the store. These men were representatives from two different coal miner's unions: the United Mine Workers Association and the newer Progressive Union. The person who was killed was with the Progressive Union and the murderer was part of the UMWA. The townspeople knew who did the killing, but he was never charged. The Progressive Miners of America was a union organized in 1932 in downstate Illinois. It was formed after United Mine Workers president, John L. Lewis, sided with coal operators and supported a contract referendum that would have reduced a miner's daily wage from six ten to five dollars.

I worked part-time in several other grocery stores around this time. I worked as a clerk at the A&P. When people came in, I would fetch the groceries they wanted and put them on the counter. This was before supermarkets, as we know them, were developed. I also worked in the butcher department of Kukandalls Grocery Store. My Uncle Carrie was the butcher there. Uncle Carrie was the exception to my drinking uncles. He married Aunt Madge, who got him to quit drinking, and as a result, he became the best of all of my mother's brothers. I also sometimes worked in the butcher department at a company store called Scott Maygatts. This store was similar to Coalfield's, which I described earlier in my story. After I came home from my service in World War II, I owned a small grocery store in Marion and used some of the skills I had learned in my high school jobs. At that time it was still difficult to get meat, so

Uncle Omar would kill a pig and give me some of it to sell. This was considered illegal because the meat had not gone through the inspection process.

Between my freshman and sophomore years of high school, when I was about fifteen, my neighbor, Conley Taylor, and I hitchhiked to Alto Pass, a town about fifty miles south of West Frankfort. We went there to get a job picking peaches in this hillier part of the state. We got hired on for two dollars per day. We slept in a barn with no bathroom facilities and bathed in a pond. We had to furnish our own food. I remember buying some lunch meat in the town, which was about one or two miles away, but our main food was the peaches. We really ate a lot of peaches during the week we were there! Also, it was very, very hot. I really felt rich when I came home with some money.

The Taylors' farm was near our farm. They were much more successful at farming than my family. First of all, they had more land and had a dairy of Jersey cattle that were tan with a little black and produced very rich milk. They had a regular milk wagon route and sold both milk and butter.

The End of High School

For the first three years, I was good about going to school. My senior year, I started hanging out at the pool hall. The owners allowed folks to sit on benches and watch people play pool without paying. I particularly liked to watch people play pool for money. One game they played was small pea pool. In this game, the numbers went up to nine. If someone got your number or if you made your own number, you collected all the money.

During my senior year, I seemed to lose interest in school, and although I was close to getting my high school diploma, I didn't think it was important at the time. To this day, I can't remember anyone asking me if I had graduated from high school.

After I was married and had a baby, I took a correspondence course in accounting from La Salle University in Chicago. I did well in this and went all the way to the auditing courses. I found that this course was a great boost to my career in later years.

CHICAGO, HERE I COME!

PART 3

(1933-34)

WINDY CITY ADVENTURES

My friend, Inman Weir, and I decided to leave West Frankfort and try looking for a job in Chicago. Inman had an aunt and uncle who lived there, and I had a friend, Joe McClarney, who had moved there with his family. Joe's divorced mother, Ma Briscoe, wrote and told me I could stay with their family when I came to the city.

In April 1933, with lodging covered, Inman and I decided to hitchhike the three hundred and twenty miles up to Chicago. Why not go for it? I had saved fourteen dollars for the trip! We met on the corner of Route 37 and Main Street and luckily soon got a ride. We managed to get picked up several more times until we reached Farina (near Champaign). We were stalled there awhile but finally got a ride up to Paxton. There we had difficulty with the hitching, so we hopped on a passenger train and tried to hide in the blinds, a space between cars. We rode this way as far as Kankakee, where a train policeman spotted us and told us to get off. We then went to the highway and started hitchhiking again. We got a ride on a cattle truck, which took us all the way to the Chicago stockyards at about 3900 South. My problem then was that Joe lived at 2000 North. For the first time, I got on a streetcar and showed the conductor the address of where I wanted to go, and he kindly told me when it was time to get off.

When I finally arrived at Joe's house, we had a good reunion because he had been gone from West Frankfort for several years. Joe instructed me in such useful information as how to jump on the platform of the elevated train from the stairs of an apartment house and completely avoid paying the fee. When I got on the train, I was able to go all over Chicago and see many new sights: giant hotels, factories, and many high-rise apartment buildings. On the south side of the city, I saw more black people than I had ever seen in my life.

After two weeks, my fourteen dollars was about gone, so I had to think about getting a job. In those days, employment agencies could sometimes get you a job. The main catch to that method was that you had to pay them some type of fee if they landed you any kind of job. After a while, an employment agency did get me a job as a flunky in a garage. I wasn't very enthused about the duties, which consisted of cleaning up after a very dirty, greasy operation. Soon after I got the job, a buddy from West Frankfort, Bill Jones, told me that they were hiring at the Swift Company's food stand at the World's Fair. Bill told me to say I was a griddle man, but when I interviewed, I got nervous and said I was a girdle man. I got the job anyway and was told I would be making the tremendous sum of eighteen dollars per week. I ended up working only one day at the garage, and that very same night I started working at the World's Fair.

WORK AND FUN AT THE 1933-34 WORLD'S FAIR

Some of the food concessions at the fair were being operated by the Swift Company (a food company contracted by the Crown Food Company, the main food provider for the fair). In the beginning week of the fair, the management had hired college students to work in the stands. They soon found that these kids weren't used to that kind of hard work and fired most of them in favor of hiring farm boys like me, who had experienced working from dawn to dusk.

We only sold four items: hamburgers, hot dogs, ham sandwiches, and coffee. The hamburgers were in frozen packages of about a dozen and were kept in new-fangled deep freezers, which were just being introduced at this time. The frozen hamburger meat looked white because it had so much fat in it. Hamburgers were our best-selling item, and I can remember cooking about fifty of them at a time. We charged ten cents for each of our four items and received many complaints from the customers about the high prices.

The stand closed at 4:00 a.m., and when I worked the night shift, I had to make sure everything was perfectly clean before I left because fair inspectors came by every day to see if the stand was in tip-top shape. This meant that we had to get grease off the ceiling, floor, and everywhere in between. We used old cake Bon Ami with hot water to do the cleaning. After the entire stand was bright and shining, we turned on a giant multicolor fan, which was beautiful. This was in keeping with the fair's theme of creating a rainbow city.

My uniform for the job consisted of a white shirt and black tie, which I had to provide. I remember the expense of getting my white shirt laundered. The company provided the white pants with green stripes down the side. We were also furnished a paper hat that was white with a green stripe.

I must have done a good job the first year because when I came back to work at the same stand in 1934, I found that I had been promoted to the job of manager with a raise to twenty-four dollars per week. In this position, I was responsible for training new employees and the general operation of the stand, which included being responsible for the inventory. I still remember the supervisor coming around on the last day of the fair in 1934 and looking the other way when some of the employees put a little of the sales money in their pockets and took some of the inventory that remained.

Both years I worked at the fair, I was able to occasionally send five dollars home to my parents. In those days, this was probably enough for them to buy a week's worth of groceries.

SIGHTS AT THE CENTURY OF PROGRESS EXPOSITION

Next month, I'll be ninety-six years old and I still smile when I talk about many of my experiences at the fair seventy-seven years ago. A definite highlight was watching Sally Rand perform her famous fan dance. I was fortunate to see her then and even a couple of times later in my life. Another experience I can vividly recall was watching the General Motors and Chrysler cars parade on the Avenue of Flags, which was located near my stand. They were assembled in plants on the fairgrounds and were beautiful, shiny, and new. I would have given anything in the world to be able to own one of those cars.

Other memories include watching the world championship horseshoe pitching contest, attending my first big rodeo at Soldier Field, and listening to big bands like Buddy Rogers and Wayne King while drinking a ten-cent beer. I also observed the famous German airship, *Graf Zeppelin*, when it flew over the fairgrounds. When I toured the Homes of Tomorrow exhibition, I saw a house made out of a brand-new product, Masonite. Later in my life, I sold extensive amounts of Masonite in lumberyards I worked in, managed, and/or owned.

I had one experience at the fair that terrified me. The stand where I worked was close to the entrance to the Sky Ride. The Sky Ride was a transporter bridge built especially for the Chicago World's Fair. One of the dirty secrets of the fair that was never reported in the newspapers was how several people committed suicide by jumping from one of the two over six-hundred-foot-high observation towers that connected the ride. Friday the thirteenth in 1933 was a day chosen for a number of these suicides. Unfortunately, that day when I was on a break, I witnessed someone jump from the tower and hit the mechanical part at the bottom where the cars of the transporter turned around. I will never forget the horrible sight of blood spattering on the white dresses and hats of nearby fair-goers. The worst memory I have is of seeing a severed foot with the shoe still on it. After I viewed that scary and sickening scene, I scurried back to work.

LIVING IN CHICAGO

I was asked by my interviewer if I was ever afraid when I lived in the big city. I do remember very clearly one incident when I was really scared. It was after midnight and I had dropped off a date on the South Side at 62nd and Halsted and was sitting on the street corner, waiting for a streetcar to take me to 62nd and South Park, which is far east of where I was. Since it was so late, the cars were not running very often. I didn't know what I was going to do, when along came a car with two guys who stopped and picked me up. When I got in the backseat, I saw all kinds of merchandise that I assumed must have been stolen. The two men had been drinking, and when they started going east down 63rd Street, they were beating on the side of the car and yelling. I was afraid that if the police stopped the car, I would be accused of having helped steal the loot. Finally, as my good luck would have it, they stopped the car and let me out right in front of my apartment.

After I moved out of Joe's house, I lived in several different apartments with three friends from West Frankfort who were all working in various jobs at the fair. Their names were Bill Manis, Bill Jones (the guy who told me about the employment opportunity at the fair), and Kenneth "Scarey" Lawrence. After we had lived together a few months, Scarey asked me when I planned to buy my own soap. It was my first realization that some household supplies weren't being furnished in our apartment. We had several different apartments together. I'll just let you guess why we moved often and in the middle of the night.

I had several girlfriends during this time. The girl I saw the most was named Sue. Sue did the same job at the fair as I did, but she usually worked at different stands. She lived far south, and when we dated, I had to ride the streetcar until the end of the line. We had some fun trips to the Indiana sand dunes, and I also had Sunday dinner with her family at her house. When asked why this relationship ended, I had to admit that it lasted until I got married.

GETTING MARRIED
AT AGE TWENTY

After the first year of the fair, I wanted to stay in Chicago but there were no jobs to be had, so around November 1, 1933, I hitchhiked back home to West Frankfort. All I remember about this hitching adventure is that I was with my roommate and buddy, Scarey Lawrence, and we got stuck somewhere in a small town and couldn't get a ride. Some kind person saw us continuing to try to thumb a ride and told us about a private home that took in people for the night; so, for a small fee, we slept in a bed for the night and successfully resumed hitchhiking in the morning. When I got home, I got back my old job with Uncle Omar. More important, I started going to the dances again and found myself dancing often with Isabel McAlpin from Marion. We had known each other casually for several years and had even double-dated when she briefly dated one of my friends, Louie Boner. At that time when Louie asked me what I thought of his date, I unenthusiastically said, "She's okay." She also had gone steady with Russell Poole, a West Frankfort basketball star. When I returned from Chicago, she had just gotten back from living in Washington, DC, for about six months.

In the winter of 1934, we started dating pretty steadily. She was pretty, liked to dance, and I had fun with her. One date that stands out occurred when there was a big snowstorm and I somehow made it the twelve miles to Marion to pick her up. When I arrived at her house, her mother said, "It's a good thing the fool-catcher is not out tonight."

April 1, 1934, I returned to Chicago and my job at the fair. As I mentioned earlier, I was promoted to the position of stand manager. In a few months, Isabel and her sister, Helen, came to Chicago to visit a friend of Helen's. It was during this visit that we started dating again, fell in love, and decided to get married. She returned to Marion in order to prepare for the wedding. After she had gone home, I began to get cold feet and wrote her to say that maybe we shouldn't get married because I wouldn't have a job after the fair was over. She wrote back and said her brother, Baker, who was very active in the Democratic Party, would be able to get me a job and that she was already making plans to get married.

When she returned to Chicago for the wedding, her folks drove her from Marion to a little town near Champaign, Villa Grove, where she took the Chicago and Eastern Illinois Railway train the remainder of the way. She and her sister, Helen, stayed with the lady from Marion who they had visited earlier in the summer. When we went to get our marriage license at the Cook County Court House, we added a few years to our ages because our friends had told us we were not old enough to get married. Although we were both twenty, I said I was twenty-four and she upped her age to twenty-three.

We called several preachers and found one on the South Side who was willing to marry us. On August 8, 1934, he performed the wedding ceremony for us in his home, which was somewhere around South 79th Street. Helen McAlpin and my friend Bill Jones stood up with us. After the wedding, we had a party at a nearby night club, where we celebrated with around ten friends by singing, dancing, and drinking. I still remember how hot it was that August night in the days before air-conditioning. We went to Mrs. Briscoe's to spend the first night of our almost seventy-two-year marriage.

Isabel Kay McAlpin Lee and Eldon Maurice Lee
on Their Wedding Night

We stayed with Ma Briscoe for a night or two and then we rented a one-room furnished apartment located on the North Side about three blocks west of Lincoln Park. Isabel tried to get a job, but couldn't find one in that Depression era. Her ideal job at that time would have been to work as a clerk in a Walgreen's drug store. During this time, she had fun with a few unmarried lady friends from Marion, attending the many movies that were available in the big city.

Soon after we were married, my employer, Crown Food Company, threw a big party downtown at the Knickerbocker Hotel for all their employees at the fair. At the party, Isabel and I both had a little too much to drink, and she wanted to take a cab home. I told her that we didn't have enough money to do that and would need to take a streetcar, which she reluctantly agreed to do. We didn't have issues with drinking in future years. I really never liked to get drunk because of the bad feeling the morning after. I probably remember this incident because when we were celebrating our thirtieth wedding anniversary at the Drake Hotel, across the street from the Knickerbocker, I saw a friend who was still working at the Knickerbocker after all those years.

In those days there were lots of things to do in Chicago for not too much money. We liked to dance at two big ballrooms, the Aragon and Trianon, where big bands played. I remember listening and dancing to Wayne King—the waltz king—and Jan Garber. At the Walnut Room in the Bismarck Hotel, I saw Perry Como singing with Ted Weem's orchestra. I knew even then that he would make it big someday. I also recall paying ten cents to see Bob Hope at the old Orpheum Theatre. He was on the stage with a beauty contest winner, Eleanor Holm, and joked about her beauty. Seeing Sammy Kaye at the Chicago Theatre was another thrill. I remember staying for the second show.

Another event of our early days of marriage in Chicago occurred when my new in-laws came to visit us and attend the World's Fair. They also brought my new wife's sixty-three-year-old aunt. It was later reported in the aunt's small town Carterville newspaper that she had been able to attend the fair at her advanced age. They all stayed with us in our small, one-room apartment. I can't exactly remember where everyone slept, but I do vividly recall that I was in the Murphy bed with my father-in-law, and I, for some unknown reason, wet the bed, which I can't recall ever doing before or since. I also added to his potential disapproval of me when he requested that I drive his car and take him to the nearby Biograph Theatre so he could see where Dillinger had recently been shot and killed. We drove there on Lincoln Avenue, which was a diagonal street, and I got lost coming home. I stopped a policeman on the corner, who told me I was going the wrong way, so I turned around and we soon arrived back at the apartment. Even after this questionable start, I got along fine with Hunter McAlpin for the remainder of his years.

Isabel and I both wanted to stay in Chicago after the fair was over, but neither one of us could find a job. We were very disappointed but felt that our best chance of finding employment was in West Frankfort, where I had friends, family, and a work history.

Around the first of October in 1934, we boarded a Greyhound bus for the trip to southern Illinois. We had to change buses and wait awhile in St. Louis. My single-life hitchhiking days were over.

YOUNG MARRIED LIFE IN SOUTHERN ILLINOIS

PART 4

(1935-44)

GETTING ESTABLISHED

When we first returned to West Frankfort, we stayed with my parents for a few months. By that time, they had moved back into the Frankfort Heights and were living on Odle Street.

My folks got along with Isabel all right, although my mother had wanted me to marry a neighbor, Ella Fay. I never cared much for Ella Fay because I felt she was too fat and unattractive. My mother liked her because she was "husky," and she thought that would make her a real hard worker. On the other hand, Mom referred to Isabel, who was thin and petite in every way, as "spindly." Ironically, Isabel was healthy most of her life and lived to ninety-two years while Ella Faye was always sickly.

I was able to get a job at Cox's Grocery Store on Main Street. It was an awful, awful job. Mr. Cox had health problems and just sat around and watched everything that went on. His wife was an old fuddy-duddy who complained all the time. I was hired to be a butcher because of my experience working for Uncle Omar. The store had no business to speak of, and I lasted there about three or four months. I quit as soon as I landed another job.

My next job was at the Stotlar-Herrin Lumber Company and was the start of my long career in the lumber business.

I got the job through the manager's wife, Ruby Kelly. I had met her when I was in high school and lived with Uncle Omar. At that time, Ruby and my Aunt Bernice were good friends and liked to kid around with me. I interviewed with Herschel Kelly; he hired me and agreed to pay me twelve dollars per week for the first two weeks. After that he raised my pay to fifteen dollars per week. We now had enough money to get our own place!

We rented an unfurnished four-room house for eight dollars a month. I remember that we had to spend another eight dollars to buy a coal-burning heating stove. We also had a gasoline cooking stove that scared us to death when it would blow up occasionally. Our budget for groceries was three dollars and seventy-five cents per week. Isabel was great at budgeting then and always. We ate a lot of Red Cross macaroni at five cents a box and hamburger that was about ten cents per pound. During the Christmas season, Isabel worked at a store called the Brokerage that bought up big lots of stuff that hadn't sold in other stores. She bought many pairs of sample shoes there because her feet were a size 4 or 5. One Christmas I bought her some pajamas at the Brokerage and just wrapped up the tops. Her parents and siblings all laughed when she opened the present.

Although I started with the title of clerk in my new job, I had varied duties. I waited on customers and sold them many items, such as wallpaper, paint, plumbing supplies, barbed wire, and lumber. I also unloaded lumber and roofing from the railroad cars. After a few months, I started driving the delivery truck sometimes. There were usually about five or six permanent employees working there, but extra help was hired to unload cement. Warder Stotlar, the son of the owner, worked with me and became a lifelong friend and a great help to my future career. Warder had just graduated from Northwestern University and his father wanted to put him in one of his five lumber yards so he could learn the ropes from the ground up. I always admired Warder because he worked as hard as I did. As I think back about my years at Stotlar-Herrin, I realize Warder was one of the best friends I have ever had. We not only kidded and had fun while at work, we also took trips to baseball games in St. Louis and did other social activities together. The people I worked with and the customers were the reasons that I really enjoyed this job.

Becoming Parents

Our life changed in several ways during the nine years I worked at the lumberyard. The arrival of a baby when we were both twenty-two was a major event. Isabel suggested we have a baby, I agreed, and about nine months later, an over eight-pound baby girl joined our family. On August 1, 1936, our daughter, Linda Jane, was born at the West Frankfort Hospital. Dr. Eldrige delivered her and must have considered it a difficult delivery because there was a ten dollar fee added to the regular twenty-five dollar charge. This was to be our only child because Isabel and I had an agreement that if the baby were a girl, we wouldn't have any more children. The other part of the deal was that if we had a boy, we might try for a girl. After attending the long, difficult forceps delivery, I decided I was satisfied with the one-child agreement.

Linda cried all night, every night, for about five weeks. This could have been caused by colic combined with the hot, hot temperatures for the first thirty days of her life—it was over 100 degrees! Of course, we didn't have air-conditioning or even a fan. As I recall, the only relief we got from the heat was opening the refrigerator and standing in front of it. I got down to about 125 pounds during this time because I couldn't sleep at night, and during the day we were hauling and unloading cement at the lumberyard. I finally slept on the back porch on a cot. We had help with the baby from Isabel's parents, Bird and Hunter McAlpin. They had three grandsons, and since Linda was the first granddaughter, she was very much admired and loved and spoiled.

Linda at Age 13 Months with Her Daddy

In 1938, Isabel and I were able to buy our first house with the help of the lumberyard. Stotlar-Herrin had stock in a building and loan company in West Frankfort, and they traded some of their stock for a five-room house at 309 South Jackson Street in town. They then sold it to me for six hundred and seventy-five dollars with a repayment deal of fifteen dollars per month and no interest. The house was about 1,100 square feet with two bedrooms, a living room, a dining room and a kitchen. I am proud of all the remodeling work I did on this house. I replaced all the windows, built cabinets in the kitchen, and painted the entire house. I did this all for very little money. For example, I built 14 feet of cabinets with ¾ inch plywood that was free because it had small defects that I was able to hide. I then painted them white and had beautiful cabinets. We also added a bathroom as soon as we could afford it.

Our Little Family in the Backyard of our
House on Jackson Street in 1940

Now that we had a house with a yard, I decided to buy chickens and raise them to eat. I only bought roosters because they were the best for frying. I put them in a brooder made with hardware cloth on the bottom and no top. Hardware cloth is metal with little squares that the chicken's feet wouldn't go through but would catch the droppings on a newspaper placed in the bottom. When it got cold, I had to bring them in the house. This didn't work too well, since when they got bigger, they got wings. One day Isabel came home from the store and there were chickens flying all over the house. Believe me, it was quite a job to catch them! After that, I put them in a fenced-in place in the yard, clipped their wings, and kept them until they got to be about one to one-and-a-half pounds; and then we started eating them. Needless to say, I was only allowed to do this project for one year. As I think back, it is ironic that I lived in a chicken house without chickens as a boy, and brought chickens into my regular house when I was grown.

In our new yard, we were able to plant a small vegetable garden with lettuce, onions, and radishes. I also had a dog pen for my bird dogs. The dog I remember most was a beautiful lemon-and-white Irish setter named Rowdy. I liked to take the dogs to my sisters' farms and quail hunting with my good friend, Burt "Chub" Jordan. Isabel and I both enjoyed eating quail. Boy was it good when she cooked it and served it with biscuits, creamed gravy, and fried potatoes!

The Beginning of World War II

On the Home Front

Like most people in my generation, I remember where I was and what I was doing on December 7, 1941, when we heard the extremely surprising news that the Japanese had bombed Pearl Harbor. It was around noon on that long-ago Sunday, and Isabel's sister, Mary Jane, and her husband, John Wilt, had come the thirty miles from Mt. Vernon to visit us when we heard the shocking news on our radio. John, a policeman, immediately said that he was going to join up. I, on the other hand, was twenty-seven, had a wife and daughter, and didn't feel any need or desire to go fight in a war.

On December 8, after Roosevelt delivered his "this is a date that will live in infamy" speech, the United States Congress voted to declare war on Japan. The only dissenting vote was cast by a Republican congresswoman from Montana, Jeannette Rankin. She was the first woman elected to serve in Congress. In a few days, on December 11, 1941, the Congress voted to join the war in Europe. Although it was widely known that we had already been sending supplies to war-torn England, Americans had resisted becoming a part of this conflict until the bombing of Pearl Harbor.

At home, the American people quickly mobilized in support of the war effort. By March of 1942, the Food Rationing Program was set into motion. Gasoline and cigarettes were also rationed and hard to obtain. We didn't have a car then, so the gasoline rationing didn't bother us except that Grandma and Grandpa (Linda called them Mom and Potsie) McAlpin had to save their gas ration stamps so they could come the twelve miles from Marion to visit Linda. Isabel and I learned to roll our own cigarettes using a little machine called a target machine. Our family was issued a war ration book. Each stamp authorized a purchase of rationed goods in the quantity and at the time designated, and the book guaranteed that each family got their fair share of goods made scarce because of the war. Rationing included all meats, butter, fat, and sugar. When I think back, I don't recall our little family experiencing any extreme hardships during this time. We learned to make do with what we could get.

The government began a massive effort to finance the war by selling war bonds. I recently read that at the end of the war on January 3, 1946, the last proceeds from the Victory War Bond campaign were deposited into the US Treasury. More than 85 million people—half the population—purchased bonds, totaling $185.7 billion. These incredible results have never since been matched. Hollywood stars were very active in promoting the sale of the bonds. Free movie days were held in theaters nationwide, with the purchase of a bond being the price of admission. Frances Dee (1909-2004) was a very famous star who came to the Strand Theatre in downtown West Frankfort. I remember getting a quick peek of her as she went into the theater.

In 1943, I quit my job at Stotlar-Herrin. The company had been unable to buy lumber unless it was to be sold for use in the war effort. For example, we could sell to the coal mines, since they were considered to be producing a product that was vital to the war. Because of these limitations, I was not getting raises and was hearing how much money the people working in war plants were making. Since there were no war plants in West Frankfort, I got a job working at the Caterpillar factory in Peoria. They were manufacturing tractors and other large equipment that was essential for the war.

Moving our family to Peoria became a story that has persisted all my life. Isabel, Linda, and I took a Greyhound bus for the half-day trip to Peoria. My in-laws had brought us fresh vegetables from their garden to take with us to our new home. The joke is that because I quit the job after only two weeks, we returned to West Frankfort on the same bus with some of the same hearty vegetables sticking out of the sacks we had brought them in. This story has been told so often that I'm not sure how much of it is exaggeration.

I vividly remember that the factory job was horrible. It was an extremely hot summertime and I worked nights, dipping red-hot piston liners into water to cool them. Hot steam hit my face and I thought I was going to burn up. I went to my supervisor and asked him for another job. The next night when I wasn't given new duties, I told them I was quitting, and they told me I couldn't quit because the job was essential to the war effort. I never went back, and nothing ever happened to me because I quit. We soon left the apartment we had rented on Main Street and headed back to West Frankfort with our same vegetables. I also remember a severe hailstorm that broke most of the glass in the downtown windows when we were living there.

If my memory serves me right, it was about this time that I worked in the Orient No. 2 coal mine for around six months. My job responsibility was to grease the loading machines with a zert gun after every shift. It wasn't a particularly difficult job and had no heavy lifting, but I quit because I hated being underground all the time. At another time, I worked for about a week at the same mine, cleaning coal cars to get them ready for loading more coal. Although I lived in an area where coal mining was the main industry, these two brief stints were enough of that business for me.

My last job as a civilian until after the war was a position as a lumberyard manager in Mt. Carmel, Illinois. I saw the job advertised in the St. Louis *Globe Democrat* newspaper and applied. E. C. Robinson Lumber Company had ten to fifteen lumber yards in Missouri, Illinois, and Indiana. I landed an interview at their home office in St. Louis. They said they were considering me because of the accounting course I had taken from La Salle University and my experience working at Stotlar-Herrin Lumber Company. I didn't get hired soon after the interview, but I got a letter about three months later saying that they wanted me to manage one of their operations in Mt. Carmel, Illinois. The company had recently purchased a lumber yard in Mt. Carmel that had been owned and operated by the same man, Mr. Mahon, for many years. When he died, his son didn't want to run the business, so he sold it to the E. C. Robinson lumber chain.

In January of 1944, our little family moved the ninety miles east to Mt. Carmel, a small town on the Wabash River. Linda was in the middle of second grade and made the first of several school changes that she would make in the next few years. We rented a house and started our new life.

My first task in my new job was to take inventory of what was left in stock after the E. C. Robinson Company had contracted to buy the business. The main customers of the yard were the oil wells in Indiana on the other side of the Wabash River. I quickly found that I was on-call to work night and day. For example, if an oil well started to come in during the middle of the night, I was expected to take a load of cement to them immediately. I would drive the truck there and, when I got into too much mud in the cornfield where they were drilling, a large Caterpillar tractor would pull me the rest of the way. I did have an employee who was supposed to drive the truck, but he lived in the country and had difficulty making it to town for the night calls. For all this work, I felt my pay was pretty meager. I didn't have to worry about this poor job choice for very long.

In April of 1944, I received my Greetings Letter from Uncle Sam, courtesy of the West Frankfort Draft Board.

My World War II Service

PART 5

(1944-46)

INDUCTION AND BASIC TRAINING

Getting my draft notice was not a big surprise. I had heard through the grapevine that the draft board in West Frankfort was running out of men and was scraping the bottom of the barrel. We old guys were all that was left. At the time I was twenty-nine and a half years old.

I immediately quit my job in Mt. Carmel and moved the family back to our house in West Frankfort. I had about a month before I had to report, so I painted the house, and Isabel arranged for her sister, Mary Jane, to come and live with her and Linda. Mary Jane's husband, John, was already serving in the army.

I received the greatest shock when I went to the train station to leave for the service. There were about sixty to sixty-five other draftees at the station with me. I knew almost every one of them because we were in the same age range and I had gone to school with most of them. Before we boarded the train, an official from the draft board got up and announced that we didn't have to go that night. It was up to us if we wanted to get on the train. The hitch was that we could still be called sometime in the future, even as soon as the very next week. I decided to go! I had already quit my job and made all of the preparations for my family. Only three men made the decision to stay. My good friend, Chub Jordan, was one of them. The three who stayed home became rich with black market activities on the home front.

When we got on the train, we went to Chicago, to the induction center, where we were given physical exams and lined up to receive our assignment to either the navy or Marines. The guy in line before me was assigned to the Marines, and I was praying that I wouldn't be going with him. I was thankful when I was sent to the navy line. I think that's where they were putting the older inductees.

We then boarded a train for boot camp. I was sent to Great Lakes, which was about fifty miles north of Chicago. I knew I was in the navy when I got my uniform, had my hair almost all cut off, suffered through many shots, and took several intelligence tests.

The worst parts of boot camp was the drilling and marching practice, the rules we were expected to follow, the bad food, and daily calisthenics. I did enjoy the camaraderie with the other fellows who were in the same boat as me. Most of the people in my company were from West Frankfort. I was fortunate to be assigned a good work detail. As luck would have it, the company clerk, Glen Thurman, was married to Melba Minton, Uncle Omar's daughter, and he picked me for the painting crew, which turned out to be an easy job. We were very slow painters and no one was supervising us very closely, so we got away with taking many breaks. The remainder of the company had to wash all of the dishes. Our painting group felt so sorry for the dishwashers that we sometimes scrub-washed their clothes for them. We all had to hand-wash and dry our white uniforms and put them under our mattress to press them.

Following the rules was very important in boot camp. For the most part, I had a good record. The old guys were usually pretty good at complying with the rules. I don't remember what I did wrong, but once I was punished for breaking a rule. The penalty for my wrongdoing was to get up every hour all night and carry a bucket of sand across a large field and back. This stupid punishment was called a piss call.

After graduation from boot camp, we got to go home for a one-week leave and show off our new uniforms. When we got a few blocks from the West Frankfort train station, the train had some kind of problem and stopped. As you can imagine, none of us could wait any longer so we jumped off the train and ran the short way to the station to see our families.

Eldon in Boot Camp at Great Lakes, Illinois

After our first leave, we returned to Great Lakes to learn about our next assignment. I was fortunate to be slated to go somewhere for further training. I was told I got this break because of my good score on the IQ tests. My friend, Scarey Lawrence, went to sea on a PT boat and survived the war. Unfortunately, a majority of the sailors from West Frankfort immediately shipped out on destroyers and lost their lives in the October 1944 Battle of the Philippines.

Advanced Training in Norman, Oklahoma

When I boarded an old WWI troop train at Great Lakes, I didn't have any idea where I was being taken. The train had an old, coal-fired engine that produced lots of soot. By the end of our journey, we had soot all over our clean, white uniforms, and we all looked like hell. The train took us through Kansas City, Missouri, sometime in the middle of the night.

After the mysterious train ride, I ended up in Norman, Oklahoma, where I was assigned to study aviation ordnance. We began our training by taking apart a .45-caliber automatic army pistol and then putting it together again. We then progressed to doing the same procedure with other guns that were used on airplanes: a .30-caliber automatic, a .50-caliber automatic, and then a 20 mm cannon. We also learned how to operate and fix cameras and bomb racks (where the bombs were held before they were released). I liked the training and worked hard so I would be able to get a good assignment after I graduated.

The weather in Norman was very, very, very hot. I particularly remember the scorching wind blowing the red dirt into our eyes and most of our other body crevices. Once, when an important admiral came, we had to drill for him in a cornfield. We were all sweating, and the red dust stuck to our uniforms. You can imagine what we all looked like!

Another memory I have from Norman is the time I pulled guard duty from midnight until 4:00 a.m. While I was standing straight up, I fell sound asleep. I was super lucky that I didn't get caught. The punishment for this lapse of duty could have been very severe.

I enjoyed the other sailors who I got to know. We didn't have classes on the weekend, so we would take a little trolley the twenty-five miles to Oklahoma City. I enjoyed eating at a good restaurant and seeing a movie on these visits. The trolley was fun to ride and only cost eighteen cents per trip.

In our barracks, we had a master-at-arms (MA) who was in charge of keeping everything under control and making sure that we all followed the rules. No one liked him because he was a hateful, grouchy old fart with some kind of a foreign accent. One night when he went to town we all ganged up and put little sand burrs with sharp stickers between his mattress cover and mattress. That night everyone in the barracks was so excited that we couldn't sleep. When he came home and went to his bed, he immediately started screaming bloody murder. We all kept our oath of silence and he never learned what had happened.

SERVING AT
JACKSONVILLE NAVAL
AIR STATION

After I graduated from ordnance school in the fall of 1944, I boarded a train for a mysterious journey to my next assignment. I figured that with my training, I would end up at sea on an aircraft carrier or at a naval air base in the States. From Norman, we went through Houston, Montgomery, Alabama, and parts of Georgia, until we arrived at Jacksonville, Florida. The most memorable part of this trip was in the train station in Houston, where I was introduced to the mushy, ground corn food called grits. We sailors from up north didn't have any idea what we were eating.

I was happy when I arrived at the Jacksonville Naval Air Base, which was located on the St. Johns River, about ten miles from the city of Jacksonville, Florida. I'll never forget the interview that determined my future in the navy. When I met with the interviewer, he had my records, which included the training I had successfully completed at Norman and my civilian work history. He asked me, "Would you like to be an inspector?"

I asked, "Is that something good?" When he answered that it was good, I told him that sounded fine with me. I always attributed this break to the good grades I had received in training and my civilian work experience. Also, he probably took my maturity into account. He then gave me some really good news: I would be stationed at the Jacksonville base for at least a year, and that meant I could bring my family down.

My inspector job was not very tough. When the guns on the airplanes had something wrong with them, they ended up in our department, which consisted of an even mixture of two hundred and fifty civilian and navy workers. When the repairs were made to the guns, they were put on a big, long table, and one of the five or six inspectors put a number stamp on them. Once I had a lieutenant who needed guns in a hurry for a plane that was leaving soon. He told me to stamp some guns before I inspected them. Even though he was a higher rank, I wouldn't put my stamp on then. When my boss came in, I told him about my decision, and he said, "Don't you worry." One of my fondest memories of this job is the smell and taste of coffee from the big urn that was somehow full all of the time. There also seemed to always be doughnuts around. Since I wasn't usually very busy, I had plenty of time to partake of the coffee and doughnuts.

Isabel and Linda Join Me

At first, the three of us stayed in a hotel in Jacksonville. Since only officers could get a pass to get off of the base, I had to forge one. Next, we moved in with a married couple on the base. I was a good friend of the guy. He had married a "Georgia Cracker" who thought Isabel could be a house cleaner for her. Isabel had gotten a job on the base soon after she arrived, so she wasn't up to doing all the work. One day when she was at work, the cracker kicked Linda and me out of the house. I believe this was one of the worst days of my life. I didn't have any money, and my family was homeless. We went to Jacksonville and found a house trailer to purchase. It cost two hundred and fifty dollars, and I called Uncle Ray Minton and asked him for some money. He went to the bank and got a loan for the trailer. It was pretty old and beat-up and was covered in a leatherette type of material that was all cracked and looked like it was from an alligator.

We moved our new home into a trailer park about ten minutes from the base. I soon covered up the ugly leatherette with Masonite, which I painted with blue paint furnished by the navy. There was no bathroom in the trailer, so we had to go to the bathhouse that was used by all of the folks in the trailer park. We cooked with a hot plate and had a heater. There was not enough electricity for us to use both of these appliances at once. There was a hurricane while we were living there. Even though I anchored the trailer, I was glad when the hurricane headed to Miami and then out to sea.

I do have some good memories from those days. At Christmas we cut down a tree, made paper ornaments for it, and put it up under the awning we had put in front of our trailer. The little town, Yukon, where the trailer park was, had a small grocery store, where we got fresh oysters and shrimp.

Isabel liked working on Corsairs at the Naval Air Station. She had to crawl out on the wings and make minor repairs. Linda caught a school bus and went to third grade at a country school. She found the school work very easy, and the teachers wanted her to skip a grade. We said no, because we figured schools in Illinois would be more difficult when we returned there after the war.

We were all happy when on August 15, 1945, we learned that the war was over! I was really relieved because it had been rumored that I was soon going to be put on a carrier and shipped to the war in the Pacific.

Going Home

Mr. Butts, the man who owned and operated the trailer park where we lived, wanted me to stay and work for him, repairing and selling trailers. We were all homesick and decided to pass up his offer. When Isabel and I were vacationing in Florida twenty-five years later, we visited the trailer park and learned that Mr. Butts had made a ton of money and owned a big home on the St. Johns River.

We weren't able to head home until January 1946. After the war was over, I passed time playing with instruments until I had enough points to get out. The navy couldn't let everyone out immediately, so they had a system of points and it took a certain number of points to be discharged. I was discharged in Jacksonville and drove home in the 1941 light blue Pontiac that we had purchased about three months before we left. This was our first car, and we were thrilled to be driving it the long distance to our *home*!

The trip home was more eventful than I had expected. First we stopped in Chattanooga, Tennessee, to visit Lookout Mountain. When we were coming down the steepest part of the mountain, I had to stop our overloaded car suddenly. Oops! The universal joint scattered all over the top of the mountain. A young kid in a car saw our plight and went down to the bottom of the mountain and sent a wrecker up to take our sad, new car down to a garage. We had to stay all night in Chattanooga while the garage repairman located and installed a new universal for us. We found a room in a private home and were on our way the next morning at about 10:00 a.m.

It started snowing the next day, and we had a flat tire in Paducah, Kentucky. I had a spare and was able to get us on our way again. As a result of all our mechanical and weather problems, we arrived at Isabel's parents' house in Marion very late at night in a snowstorm. We were glad to finally be back to our home in Little Egypt.

Dad passed away peacefully on March 31, 2010, a couple of weeks after he told me about his World War II experience. Please join me as I tell some more stories about his life.

AS WE SAT

By Linda Lee Ream

I will always remember the year I sat with Dad while he told me stories of his young life.

He spoke from his heart more than from his head, as he sometimes squirmed because of the pressure of painful sores.

His eyes sparkled as he remembered the fun he had when he was young and roamed around the neighboring family farms completely on his own.

He relived the pain of stepping on white-hot coals and burning his little three-year-old feet.

A big smile was on his face while he talked about food and remembered the delicious taste of the rabbits that Jack caught.

His voice was filled with delight when he told me about scavenging for materials to construct his only toys.

I could hear the sorrow he was feeling when he described his brother's illness and the great sadness it brought to the entire family.

The love that he felt for his parents was evident as he told me that they were good people and not demanding of him in any way.

When I asked him about his best memories, he told me, with pride in his voice, about his many achievements in his career and all of his accomplishments and happy times at the Gardens, his assisted living home where we sat and visited.

The times I sat and listened to my dad's life stories brought me closer to him than I had ever been in all my life.

I am so thankful that we had the opportunity to be together and relive part of his wonderful life.

As I summarize the rest of his life, I will imagine that he is continuing to talk with me and will try my best to capture his true character and personality.

THE REST OF THE STORY

(1946-2010)

By Linda Lee Ream

WORK

A Satisfying Career

Dad appeared happy and content throughout the remainder of his long life. He worked, loved, and enjoyed life in a balanced way that was a shining example to those of us fortunate enough to observe and learn from him.

As with many returning World War II servicemen, Dad had no job waiting for him when he got back to West Frankfort in January 1946. He had developed a strong work ethic growing up in Little Egypt and had learned to take any job he could get to earn money for his family. First, he got a sales job with his uncle, Ray Minton, who owned an appliance store. He sold various appliances, including a new-fangled electric clothes washer. I remember he brought home one of these miracle machines for Mother to use. It had two tubs, and the idea was to put the clothes in one tub for washing, and when that was done, the clothes were placed in the second tub for the spin-dry cycle.

This job lasted for a couple of months and then my folks found an opportunity in Marion, a town about twelve miles south of West Frankfort, where my maternal grandparents lived. They bought a house with a small grocery store next door. Dad ran the store for a couple of years but didn't like being confined in such a small space. He then purchased a truck and traveled around selling candy and cigarettes to neighborhood grocery stores.

In 1949, he got his first big career break. He became the manager of a lumberyard in Alexander, Illinois, a farm town of about two hundred and fifty people in central Illinois. By the beginning of 1950, our little family had moved to Alexander which was twenty miles west of Springfield, Illinois. We were no longer in Little Egypt, but Dad brought with him the entrepreneurial skills that he had honed since he started his shoeshine business at the tender age of twelve. He eventually became a partner/owner at the Crawford and Calhoun lumberyard and spent thirty-three successful years there until he retired in 1982.

For several years, Dad was the leader in the United States, selling packaged pole-frame construction. He was interviewed for an article in the 1959 *Illinois Building News* and told them his methods for selling pole buildings. The magazine printed, "He knows he must make the first move in many instances. The customer may be a bit slow about recognizing needs. Consequently, he will take a farm customer on an inspection to see some pole buildings sold by his dealership. Much of his sales work depends on his taking the lead. He talks pole buildings at every opportunity. He talks the flexibility of pole buildings, for they can be used for housing livestock, storing feed, equipment, fertilizer or other items."

Dad Accepting the First-Place Award for Selling the
Most Doane Pole Buildings in the Country

Dad held many leadership positions in the business community. He was president of the Alexander Business Association from 1955 to 1960. He was also president of the Sawdust Club, an organization of lumber dealers in central Illinois who met once a month to discuss common problems and solutions. He discussed farm buildings on prestigious panels for the Illinois Lumber Dealers Association and the University of Illinois School of Agriculture.

LOVE

Isabel

Mother was the love of Dad's life. He told me he married her because she was pretty, petite, and a good dancer. He then added, with a twinkle in his eye, "I was in love with her." My parents had the same basic family and life values, but very different personalities. Mother was shy while Dad was extremely outgoing and never met a stranger.

My memories of growing up were of a loving couple who I didn't see fight or even disagree. Dad was very affectionate and would often go up and kiss Mother while she was working in the kitchen.

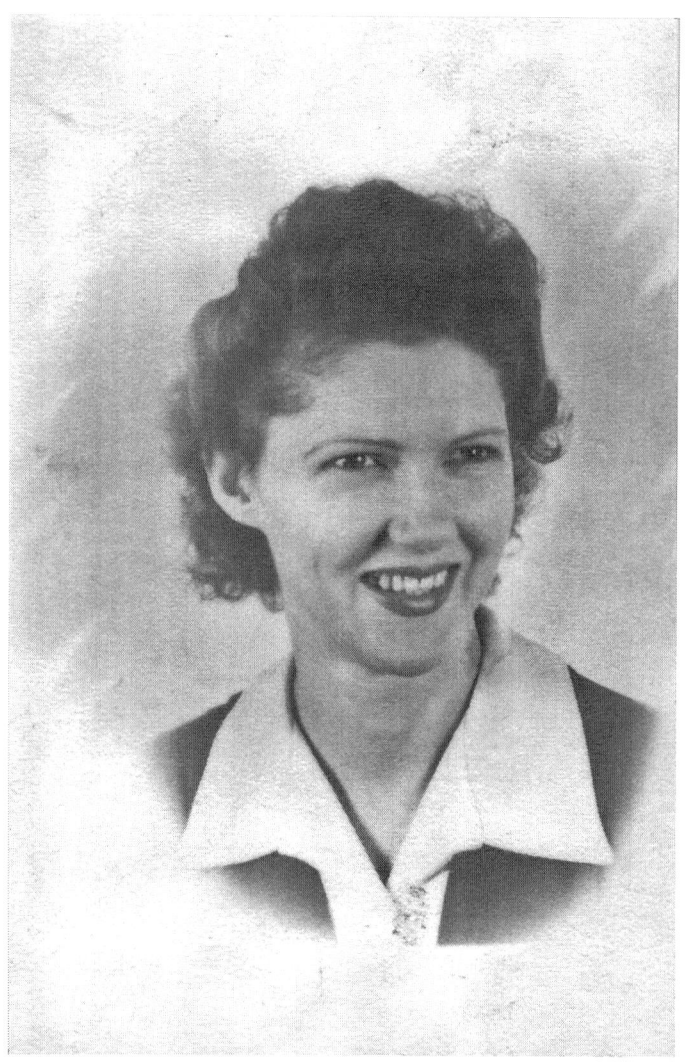

Isabel in about 1944

Mother was a homebody, a loyal wife, and she always wanted people to know that she was a Democrat and a Chicago Cubs fan. Dad agreed with her on both of these issues. She preferred to socialize with her sisters and their families, and that's what they did. Dad seemed to do what she wanted without her ever having to tell him. He let her make decisions about the small stuff, but when it came to making a living, he was in charge. For example, he made the decision to take the job in Alexander even though she didn't want to move. Mother didn't like living there because it was very small and she found it difficult to meet new people. The only good part of the move for her was being closer to her sister, Helen, and her family who lived in Springfield. She gave in to physical "female" problems during these years, and I remember her not feeling well during most of my high school years.

In the early sixties, after I was married, they moved to Springfield, and Dad commuted to Alexander for work. They met several couples there, played lots of bridge, and even took short trips with some of their new friends.

Dad showed his true devotion to his long-time wife when he solely took care of her the last fourteen months of her life when she was suffering from dementia due to small strokes she had endured in her last years. When she died on Mother's Day in 2006, after almost seventy-two years of marriage, he said, "I want to get in that bed and go with her."

Seventieth Wedding Anniversary in 2004

My Life with Daddy

When I look back, I think I must have been the luckiest girl in the entire world! I had kind, loving parents, and my high school years were in the golden era of the fifties. My generation was called the Silent Generation, which was squeezed between the WWII Greatest Generation and the rebellious young folks of the sixties. It was a simple and quiet time of conformity, in my experience.

I have a potpourri of memories from those years. Our house in Alexander was small, with only four rooms. My folks purchased a television set in 1952 that became their main source of entertainment. I could never understand how they could sit and watch the wrestling matches on the snowy TV. I remember wearing rolled-up jeans with white ship-n-shore blouses, and saddle shoes with white bobby socks. Of course, at school I followed the conservative, unspoken dress code and always wore dresses.

I didn't realize until I left home that my daddy was so special. He was a kind man who listened to me without being critical. He had a wonderful sense of humor and approached life with a positive attitude. He didn't lecture me or lay down any rules. I was on my own to do the right thing.

The only time I can remember him getting angry with me was when I was fifteen and he was teaching me how to drive. Since we lived in the country, he took me to learn on the blacktop and gravel roads. During one driving lesson, he told me to turn, and I didn't respond quickly enough and drove the car straight in a ditch. We were both scared, and he yelled at me because he was frightened. A nearby farmer who Daddy knew came and pulled the car out of the ditch. About forty-five years later, we ran into the farmer and his wife in a restaurant in Springfield. The farmer asked, "Is this the daughter who went in the ditch?" Dad really thought this was funny and laughed every time we recalled the story from then on. When Dad was ninety-four and lived in Colorado, he and I took a driving trip back to Little Egypt so he could visit his sister, Lura, who was ninety-seven at the time. He didn't criticize my driving once, but got a big laugh when I was stopped, for the first time in my life, in the middle of Kansas for speeding.

I always tried to please my parents but was still able to have lots of fun. In my small high school, I was a big fish in a little pond. I was a cheerleader, held class offices, was elected homecoming queen, played flute in the band, and earned stellar grades. In retrospect, I believe I was able to have such a good high school experience because I was striving to emulate my dad's habit of being friendly and caring to everyone he met. He taught me that:

> Nobody is better than you are,
> And you aren't better than
> Anyone else.

I think Daddy was the most proud of me when I was awarded a Morgan County scholarship to the University of Illinois. At the time, I didn't think it was a big deal because all I did was take a test and receive one of the five scholarships that the county gave for tuition. He was still remembering this when he was in his nineties and in an assisted-living facility. He wrote in the in-house newspaper that his happiest memory of Thanksgiving was of me coming home from the U. of I., where I had a scholarship.

My daddy and I had mutual respect and admiration from those high school years until he passed away. In later years, we would refer to each other as perfect. He was the perfect father, and he told me I was the perfect daughter.

Dad's Day at the Kappa Delta Sorority in 1956

THE FAMILY GROWS

My sophomore year in college, I met a young architecture student, Bruce Ream, who was from Rockford, Illinois. After a few months of dating, he gave me his fraternity pin, which in those days meant that we were engaged to be engaged. My folks liked Bruce well enough but were disappointed that I wasn't finishing my education. They were pleased when I finally got my college degree twenty years later and four years after that earned my master's degree in Counseling from the University Of Northern Illinois.

Our family has an often-told story about Bruce's first visit to our home in Alexander. As I mentioned before, we had a small house and there was no place for Bruce to sleep when he came over soon after we were pinned. We didn't even have a full-sized couch in the living room that would fit his six-foot body. We did have an old-fashioned breezeway between the house and the garage, so my parents decided to purchase a metal glider for him to sleep on in this screened-in passageway. During the night when he was sleeping, we had a terrible storm with wind, rain, and close lightning. As Bruce tells the story, no one in the house came out to check on him during the night. He says that the next day, Dad opened the door and nonchalantly asked, "How'd you sleep, Bruce?" In later years when we asked Dad if this was a test for his future son-in-law, he just grinned and gave a little chuckle. Dad told this story at Bruce's fiftieth birthday party, and Bruce repeated it at Dad's Celebration of Life program.

Dad always respected Bruce because he became a registered architect, worked hard, and was a good husband and father.

A few days before he died, Dad said, "I have had a good relationship with my son-in-law for fifty-three years."

Ten months after we were married, Tamara Jane arrived on Christmas Day, 1957. On June 9, 1962, we added Julie Kay, and Todd Bruce arrived soon after on May 8, 1963. Dad loved and enjoyed his three grandchildren, and they adored him. Even though we lived in Rockford, a city about two hundred miles north of Springfield, our family managed to get together with my folks every six to eight weeks. We were together, usually in Rockford, to celebrate almost all the holidays: Christmas, Thanksgiving, Mother's and Father's Days, and the kids' birthdays. Bruce's parents, Margaret (Marg) and Roy Ream, and his little sister, Jann, who was only four when we got married, joined us for these special times. My dad and Roy hit it off from the very beginning because they had the lumber business in common. Roy worked as a salesman at a local lumberyard in Rockford, and Bruce had worked at the same yard for several summers. All three men enjoyed getting together and having lively conversations about the happenings at their respective lumberyards. Many years after Roy and Dad retired, there was still a lot of discussion about the outrageous price of redwood.

Todd, Linda, Tamara, Bruce, and Julie
(left to right) in the Late Sixties.

In later years, his grandchildren presented him with two great-grandchildren each.

Tamara's boys:

Isaiah Lee O'Rear—April 21, 1981
Zachary Ream Schafft—December 17, 1986

Julie's boys:

Nicholas Adam Lowry—August 18, 1984
Benjamin Anthony Lowry—January 17, 1987

Todd's twins:

Catherine Lee Ream—August 4, 2007
Charles Todd Ream—August 4, 2007

Four Great-Grandsons in 2000—
(left to right) Nick, Isaiah, Ben, and Zach

FUN AND JOY

FINDING JOY IN THE SMALL THINGS

Dad appeared to find pleasure in life no matter what he was doing. The simple things made him content and happy. For example, he could sit for hours and talk with his beloved brother-in-law and best friend, Harry Hagel, Aunt Helen's husband. Uncle Harry told what he referred to as "shaggy dog stories," which were long, rambling jokes involving unreal or irrational behavior and usually having an irrelevant conclusion. The two men told and retold family tales that made them laugh. They never put people down in their stories but had a knack for making you feel special. I know this because many of their tales were about me when I was growing up.

Dad thoroughly relished meeting new people, starting a conversation and listening carefully to what the new friend had to say. When he passed away, I heard many times from people he did business with, such as bank tellers and insurance agents, that they didn't know him well but he always made them feel special. When he moved to Colorado and lived in an assisted-living home with about one hundred people, he often mentioned how much he liked learning their histories.

Dad always enjoyed having a new car, especially a Chrysler. Maybe that was a throwback to his days of seeing the sparkling new autos when he was nineteen and working at the World's Fair. As I remember, Chryslers were the only vanity purchases that he made.

He and mother liked to take road trips all over the country. They traveled to all of the lower forty-eight states, except North Dakota. In later years, he astonished us all with his ability to remember the route numbers on the trips that he had taken fifty or sixty years before. He was still driving until a month before he died.

All of his life, Dad was a keen follower of several sports. I remember he always told me the scores of the University of Illinois basketball and football teams. He was a lifelong fan of Chicago Cubs baseball (although they never won a pennant in his lifetime) and Chicago Bears football.

Bridge was Dad's card game of choice. He was an excellent bridge player who knew the rules, but was very intuitive and had a sixth sense when playing the game. He was in a couple's bridge club and a men's club during many years in Springfield. Unfortunately, by the time Mother passed away, all of his bridge friends had died. He was very happy when he moved to Colorado and was able to play bridge while living at the Gardens at Columbine.

Throughout his life, Dad enjoyed listening to many types of music, and when he was a young man, and also in his last years, he had fun dancing. He told me about having an Edison wind-up phonograph when he was a young boy in West Frankfort. I have a sketchy memory of always having some type of phonograph that played records. Through the years, the record players got better sound. In the fifties, audio manufacturers began to use the term "high fidelity" to describe records and equipment that provided a more faithful sound reproduction. In the nineties, my folks had a stereophonic (stereo) sound set, which created some semblance of live orchestral performers by having the listener sit in the middle of two loudspeakers. Their stereo was housed in a large wooden console that their bank gave them when they deposited a certain amount of money in the early nineties.

In the last decade of his life, Dad had a boombox. This is a portable stereo system that is capable of playing AM/FM radio stations, cassettes, and CDs. I can still see him listening to his CDs with his eyes closed when he was in his room at the Gardens.

He told me how important dancing was to him when he was a young man going with his many friends to night clubs, where he danced to the big bands that played in Little Egypt. He had a graceful dancing style and he remembered that all the girls wanted to dance with him. As you recall, he and Mother met and courted at dances.

He loved every opportunity he got to dance during the last four years of his life. Periodically, the assisted-living facility brought in bands that had the sound of the big bands of the thirties and forties. When he called me New Year's Day of 2010, he was very excited about the party he had attended the afternoon before. He told me he danced with many lady residents and members of the staff and that the old people abandoned their canes and walkers and had a great time dancing! This was only three months before he died at the age of ninety-six and a half!

THE LAST CHAPTER

FOUR MORE GOOD YEARS

MORE NEW BEGINNINGS

Shortly after Mother died, we asked Dad if he would come and live near us in the Denver, Colorado suburbs. It didn't take him long to say yes because most of his family and friends in Springfield had either died or moved away. He also emphasized that he wanted to be close to us and his grandchildren, Todd and Julie, who lived in the Denver area. He quickly started getting ready for the move by employing a realtor to sell his duplex/townhouse and selling his furniture and household goods himself. He got all of his customers to come by word of mouth. He put on his old salesman's hat and got a real kick out of negotiating and selling his possessions at good prices. The realtor sold his home to the first person who looked at it.

The last week of June, only six weeks after Mother's death, we drove to Springfield to do a final clean-up of Dad's house and bring him back to Colorado with us. He wanted to take only his giant TV and recliner with him. We rented a small U-Haul and took off on old Route 36 for his new home.

Although Dad put up a good front for us, I could tell that he was sad as we drove along the highway that he and Mother had taken many times through the years on vacations—to visit Todd in college at Gunnison, Colorado, and, in the last several years, to see us.

When we arrived in Colorado, Dad said he wanted to go straight to his new assisted-living home. We had rented him a one-bedroom apartment at the Gardens of Columbine, a lovely place in Littleton only ten minutes from our Highlands Ranch home. As we were walking up to the front door, Dad took my hand and said, "I don't know a soul in there." I was very relieved when he started joking with the nurses, who gave him his entrance physical examination shortly after his arrival. He called me after his first full day at the Gardens and was excited about the new friends he met and the big, delicious breakfast he had been served. I then dared to feel that he would be happy in his new home.

After a few weeks, the assistant activity director pulled me aside and told me that Dad's kindness and good attitude were having an amazingly positive effect on the other residents. This was the first of many stories of his leadership and friendship that I would hear about from the staff and residents of the Gardens.

HONORS AND LEADERSHIP

Dad was very proud of the honors and recognition he received during his last years. Shortly before Valentine's Day 2007, I got a call from the activity director telling me that the residents had elected Dad the Valentine's Day king, and his lady friend, Dorothy, had been chosen to be the queen. He was ecstatic when he received his crown and had a swell time dancing with Dorothy at the party afterward. I was glad that he had recently purchased new dentures, since he was flashing his attractive smile for everyone to see.

Valentine's Day King in 2007

In the last two years of his life, he was elected by his housemates to serve as president of the Residents' Council. He loved acting as the liaison between the facility management and the residents. He also started and chose the participants of a group of about eight of the most highly functioning and intelligent residents. He called these folks the CORE Group. This select group got together in the private dining room every other week and discussed changes they would like to see. Dad took this information to the appropriate management person for consideration. He also invited guest speakers to tell about their current or preretirement jobs. Some of these speakers were employees of the Gardens who explained their roles in the operation of the facility. He also invited others, including Julie, Todd, and me, to talk about their past and present careers.

My father created and implemented several in-house programs that he hoped would enhance the lives of the participants. In his first year in residence, he started a music hour and played CDs of all types of music: classical, country, big band, fifties, and sixties (he loved Elvis Presley). Although the activity director had told him that this type of entertainment had been tried before and failed, Dad did it anyway and his efforts were rewarded with good attendance and praise of his idea. He became known as the resident DJ.

Probably his most appreciated accomplishment was the in-house newsletter he started writing in 2008. It was entitled *Letter to the Residents from Eldon Lee*. For the newsletter, he interviewed other residents and invited employees of the Gardens to write guest columns. He also told about the organized activities he attended and shared his feelings about the happenings in the small world of his assisted-living home. Reflecting his positive personality, the newsletter was supportive and uplifting for all who read it.

In 2008, while watching his lady friend, Dorothy, die a peaceful death under hospice care, Dad became friends with the hospice caregivers who were contracted to work in-house with terminally ill residents. He decided that the families of the residents should learn about this process, and initiated and helped coordinate six informational sessions for residents and their families. Bruce and I attended one of these sessions to increase our knowledge of hospice care. Dad's desire was to die at the Gardens with end-of- life hospice care, and he wanted us to know more about the process. His plan worked well because we were prepared to arrange for hospice comfort care at the end of his life.

Dad had a special way of enlisting the help of others, including me, for his programs. He had an idea to give refresher bridge training for folks at the Gardens who hadn't played in many years. He suggested that I come over and teach these sessions. Since I'm not a very avid bridge player, I got two friends in my bridge club who were excellent at bridge to take turns leading these sessions. I always attended and played during these monthly Tuesday morning games, and my friends and I enjoyed lunch afterward with Dad and the other players.

Bruce was also called on to share his radio-controlled model airplane hobby by bringing his airplanes in to show the residents and demonstrating them in flight at the flying field his club used. We also presented a program of photos from a trip we took to Japan.

Dad with His Grandchildren at the Gardens
Julie, Todd, and Tamara (left to right)

BUSY, BUSY, BUSY

Dad got a kick out of participating in the in-house exercise classes: Stretch and Flex and Yoga for Seniors. He also liked the local trips that the staff planned. These included going out to lunch, viewing Christmas decorations, and even experiencing a ride on the Denver RTD light rail system.

He really got excited when he told me about the trips they took in the mountains where he could observe the beautiful Colorado scenery. Although Dad was never interested in gambling, he loved going to Blackhawk, an old mining town where the state allows gambling. He told me he went because of the gorgeous scenery and the large buffet lunch.

When the group took two field trips to Georgetown, a historic town beside I-70, about forty minutes west of

Littleton, Dad was delighted when he was able to ride on the Loop Railroad that operates there. He told me a story about the first time the group visited. It seems that Dad's friend, John, had a problem that made him need to use the restroom frequently. Dad selflessly offered to stay with him and miss the train ride, although he was very eager to experience it. Fortunately, one of the activity directors said she would stay with John.

It always made me nervous when my adventurous father took off in his silver Chrysler on road trips to the mountains. One time he drove his lady friend, Dorothy, and another couple two hours southwest of Littleton to show them our mountain house in Hartsel, Colorado. He said he didn't take them inside the house because he was the only one who was physically able to walk up the stairs. He also liked to take his buddies on the forty-minute drive into the mountains to eat at Hog Heaven, his favorite restaurant on Route 285.

Bruce and I enjoyed taking Dad to our home in the mountains, situated at an altitude of 9,200 ft. He said he liked just sitting there and listening to the sound of silence. We spent many hours there, reminiscing about old times and his exciting experiences at the Gardens of Columbine.

Bruce and Dad at Our Mountain Home in Hartsel, Colorado

One of the highlights of his adventures in the mountains happened when Joy and Charlie Cash, his niece (Lura's youngest daughter) and her husband visited him. He wrote in the October 2008 in-house newsletter: *"The day before the bus trip to Echo Lake, I had guests drop in from Benton, Illinois. They wanted to see the mountains in full color, and we sure did. We followed the bus up to Echo Lake. That is 10,600 ft. up to Mt. Evans. We departed from following the bus and went over to Georgetown and had lunch at The Happy Cooker. From there we went over Guanella Pass at 11,800 ft. and on to Grant on Hwy 285, then back to Littleton. I think we hit the perfect time to see the Aspen at the height of their golden beauty. At times it seemed the whole mountainside was gold trimmed in green. My niece said she had a wonderful day. She had to stop many times to take pictures, and I know she sure got some beautiful shots."*

Dad was able to celebrate the holidays and other special occasions with his family in the Denver area. When he told me his life story, he said that he didn't remember ever having a birthday party as a child. Well, Bruce and I really wanted to make his ninety-fifth birthday special. We reserved the large activity room at his assisted-living home and invited all the residents, plus our friends who had gotten to know him. There were around one hundred people at his party. The following is the article he wrote in the October 2008 newsletter about the party: *"Maybe once in a lifetime, a person feels he is the luckiest person on the face of the earth. That's the way I felt Sunday afternoon from 2 to 4 p.m. at my birthday party. I'd like to thank Linda and Bruce for a job well done. I know it was not easy. If you did not attend the party, you missed a rare treat. My great-grandchildren were here (one-year-old twins), a boy and a girl. Their names are Charlie and Catherine. By the way, Charlie will give you a high-five if you just ask him."*

Todd, Charlie, Catherine, and Dad at the
Ninety-Fifth Birthday Celebration

DYING WITH DIGNITY

Dad taught those around him the right way to die, just as he had showed us all how to live. Around the time of the holidays in 2009, Dad told me that food no longer appealed to him. This was sad, because he had enjoyed eating throughout his life. About six weeks before his death, he started complaining about a severe stomach ache that he had mostly after he ate breakfast. This pain would usually diminish after an hour or so.

His doctor sent him for a series of tests and then called us in to his office to tell us the results. Dad, Bruce, and I got the news that we had dreaded. Dr. Mike told us that Dad had untreatable colon cancer. Because it was terminal, he suggested that he begin hospice care. Dad's reaction was, "I guess my warranty has run out."

Dr. Mike replied, "You had the extended warranty."

We all went back to the Gardens and began the process of putting my beloved father in the hands of the hospice team: nurses, a social worker, and a clergyman. He passed away peacefully twelve days later on March 31, 2010.

When he found out his condition was terminal, he wanted to let the other residents know why he had started on the hospice program, so he wrote the following note.

To All My Friends Here at the Gardens

My time here at the Gardens, I believe, has been one of the happiest, most rewarding times of my life.

Now, the doctors have diagnosed me with cancer, which means I won't be around for much longer. So I will be giving up the monthly newsletter and CORE Group meetings.

*It has been a distinct pleasure spending these last years here with all of you nice people. My last advice—*don't *lose your sense of humor!*

Yours,
Eldon Lee

CELEBRATION OF A LIFE WELL-LIVED

As I was leaving Dad's room a few months before he died, he handed me a small envelope with a piece of paper detailing what he wanted for his *Celebration of Life* program to be held in the Activity Room at the Gardens. He emphasized to me that he wanted everyone to have a good time without any tears. He also requested that some of his favorite songs from the fifties and sixties be played and that we serve real wine or champagne.

Opening Prayer
  Rev. Roy Adams from the Littleton United Methodist Church Care Team

"How Great Thou Art"
  Elvis Presley

Memories of My Dad
  Linda Ream

Meditation
  Rev. Adams

Poems
  Randall Davidson

A Grandson's View
  Todd Ream

Remembering Eldon
  Friends in the Audience

"Make the World go Away"
  Eddie Arnold

Toast to Eldon
  Bruce Ream, Son-in-law

Closing Prayer
  Rev. Adams

Light Refreshments and Fellowship

Eldon Lee: A Celebration of Life, Sunday, April 18, 2010

TODD'S NOTES FOR HIS EULOGY AT HIS GRANDPA'S CELEBRATION OF LIFE SERVICE

My name is Todd Ream. I'm Eldon's grandson. He was always Grandpa Lee to me.

I'm under specific instructions from him to keep this talk happy and cheerful, so here we go.

Wow, what a grandpa he was!

1) He was a great grandpa to my sisters, Tamara and Julie, and to me.
2) He was a great husband to my grandmother, Isabel.
3) He was a great father to my mother, his only child, Linda.
4) He was a great father-in-law to my father, Bruce.
5) And he was super great-grandfather to my nephews, Ben, Nick, Isaiah, Zackary, and finally, my own two-and-a-half-year-old twins, Catherine and Charlie.

In short, he was a rare, super-high-quality individual with the kind of attributes we all aspire to have, but sometimes fall short.

Grandpa Lee never seemed to fall short himself.

Growing up observing my grandfather made me a better person. I can't talk about all of his positive attributes today because there is just not enough time.

But I did want to take this opportunity to talk about a few of the quality attributes I observed as a child and an adult.

LOYALTY

Grandpa was married to my grandmother over seventy years. Wow, that's loyalty!

But I think during the marriage, he might have said no to her maybe three times, tops.

In fact, when I got married, he pulled me aside and said, "I'm going to give you some advice." He told me there are only two words you need to know to make your marriage work. Those two words were "yes, dear."

He told me if you get that down, you will be married as long as he had been. If you ask my wife, she will tell you I'm not as good at it as Grandpa was, but I do try.

My grandpa did everything for my grandmother. She didn't even drive a car.

When she needed to go to the supermarket for double coupon senior citizen Tuesdays, he drove her.

When she wanted to go to the mall, he took her and simply either waited for her in the car or sat down on a bench in the mall.

I logged some hours in the car with Grandpa and my dad, waiting for my grandmother to finish her shopping.

He never complained; he just patiently waited for her to return.

Then later in life, when my grandmother became ill, my grandfather, who was over ninety years old, took care of her for over a year and half, all by himself.

Without a selfish bone in his body, never complaining, never asking anyone else for help, without ever giving it a second thought, he had 100 percent dedication and loyalty to my grandmother.

MAKING FRIENDS

Another great attribute: he was able to make a friend anytime/anywhere. What a quality!

He never judged anyone. He didn't care if you were the president of a major corporation or an auto mechanic—he was going to treat you the same: with respect.

I bet there is no way to count the number of random strangers who had encounters with my grandpa, either sitting on a park bench, waiting on a bench in the mall, or standing in line at a bank.

If you were lucky enough to meet him, you were always going to leave with a smile on your face, knowing you had just made a new friend and met a wonderful person.

I remember when we took Grandpa to burro days in Fairplay, Colorado. It's a local celebration where they race burros up the mountain, and after the race is complete, there is a small town parade.

Well, Grandpa was very excited about the entire event, so before the parade started, we put him in a chair along the parade route and went to get some food. We all came back about five minutes later; of course, he had already made a good friend in the lady who was sitting next to us.

He broke the ice by commenting on her burro earrings, and within five minutes he knew more about her than most people know about people they have worked with for years. He even knew the mode of transportation she took to the parade, which happened to be a motorcycle.

ALWAYS OPTIMISTIC

He was always definitely a "glass half full" kind of a guy. It was very rare to see him in a bad mood. He was consistently optimistic and he loved life and people.

I remember the day he moved into the Gardens. My grandmother had just passed away. He had just sold most of his belongings. He had just had a two-day car trip across the county.

He was in a new home. He didn't know anyone. And he was in a new city.

For most people this could be a bummer—but not for Grandpa.

We had just moved his last belongings into his apartment. We were finally sitting, when one of the residents knocked on the door once and came flying into the room with his walker.

This resident introduced himself and saw that Grandpa had a bag of homemade peanut brittle sitting on his kitchen counter. It was a farewell gift from his former neighbor in Springfield.

He asked if he could have a piece. Grandpa, of course, said yes, and at this point the man took the entire bag of peanut brittle, put it on his walker, and started down the hall.

As he walked away, he started mumbling that he wasn't supposed to eat it because of his diabetes. I said, "Grandpa, that guy just took your peanut brittle," and Grandpa replied, "That's okay; don't worry about it."

With his characteristic positive outlook on life, Grandpa looked at the next phase of his life here at the Gardens as an opportunity to meet new people, make new friends, and go places he had never gone before.

The next morning after he had his peanut brittle lifted from his room, he went down to breakfast and immediately made four new friends, and that was just the beginning of his three and a half year stay at the Gardens. Some of his accomplishments here included:

1) Being elected the Valentine's Day king.
2) Serving as president of the Residents' Association.
3) Founding the "Music by Eldon" hour

4) Starting and leading the Resident CORE Group.
5) Implementing and writing the newsletter.

GREAT SENSE OF HUMOR

He was truly a funny guy who loved to laugh. He had a dry, witty, sophisticated sense of humor, and some people say it's where I got my own sense of humor.

I remember as a kid going down to visit my grandparents in Springfield, Illinois. Much of our time was spent laughing. What a great way to go through life!

His one-liners were classic. After meeting a new lady friend who lived a few doors down from him, he took me aside and said, "Todd, we are wearing out the carpet between the two rooms."

He also thought it was super funny during his last Christmas dinner when my son counted to three and then threw a big chunk of food that ended up sticking to the wall behind him. He laughed for days about it.

He had the wisdom to know that the best way to go through life was laughing about it. As he wrote in his final letter to the residents at the Gardens, "You need to keep your sense of humor." I think we can all learn a lot from that. I know I did.

As you all know, my grandfather was a wonderful person and he touched everyone in this room in a positive way.

He was a class act, the type of person who it is a privilege to meet, and throughout my entire life I have been very proud and happy to have had the privilege to call him my Grandpa.

A few weeks after his Celebration of Life in Colorado, we went to Illinois for a small burial service. His ashes were placed next to Mother's on a beautiful little hill just across the road from the tomb of Abraham Lincoln in Oak Ridge Cemetery.

MORE MEMORIES OF A GOOD MAN

Dad was a self-made man who was kind, gentle, and considerate of those around him. He always had a smile and a kind word for everyone. He will be greatly missed, and, I believe, his spirit will live on in the hearts of those who knew and loved him.

The Author and Her Grandson, Isaiah

MEMORIES OF ELDON LEE BY HIS GREAT-GRANDSON

ISAIAH LEE O'REAR

I was fortunate that I was able to know my great-grandfather for three decades. He first visited me shortly after I was born in 1981, and I last visited him shortly before his death in 2010. Even before he visited me, my mother gave me his last name as my middle name. In reading Eldon's memories of his own youth, it is probably fitting that I was not given Eldon as a first name. Eldon said that when he was young, he wished he had a more normal name. Like Eldon, when I was young I also wished I could have a more normal name than my first name, so I went by my middle name in most of elementary school.

As I was growing up, my parents moved frequently, and I also moved frequently from one parent to the other. I pretended that each new place was a new planet, and that I was an intrepid explorer. Every year my grandparents would fly me into Chicago to visit. I would pretend that I was returning to Earth from the alien worlds.

My grandparents were very good about making sure I had a chance to see my four great-grandparents almost every year. From Chicago, we drove to see the Reams in Rockford or the Lees in Springfield, or the great-grandparents would come to Chicago.

From my first visit to my last visit, Great-Grandpa Lee always said that I could grow up to be president (in 2032, he estimated). He thought of history in terms of presidents.

Great-Grandpa had absorbed the local legend of Abraham Lincoln. He remembered the inauguration of FDR, and rooted for all subsequent Democrats based on FDR's politics. He visited the presidential libraries and historical sites. Although it is very unlikely that I will become president, his belief in the possibility made me feel connected to this country and its history.

He could easily recount the past. When I moved to some out-of-the-way town, he would tell me about his trip to that town fifty years ago. Despite his detailed, memory, he did not indulge in nostalgia. One time at a family picnic, I brought out the VHS camera and asked him if he could tell me about the good ol' days. That was in 1998, at the height of the swing music revival, and I hoped to hear about big bands and zoot suits. He responded, "The good ol' days are now."

He was not fearful of technology, and he lived to see the VHS camera made obsolete by my smartphone. He was always excited to see what they came up with next. During his last year living in Springfield, I made an overnight visit. After a day of sightseeing, I had difficulty sleeping, so I went to the kitchen to grab some leftovers from our restaurant visit earlier that day. I had ordered the Horseshoe, a local dish made up of an open-faced sandwich topped with cheese fries. He slept upright in his lazy chair, and he woke up, and we had chance to talk through the night. We talked about contemporary politics. The world had changed, but his principles hadn't: the goal of life is to make an honest living, and the goal of politics is to ensure everyone has the opportunity to make an honest living. He saw a century of social change but did not fear it or think about trying to turn back the clock to some simpler time. He said he "didn't give a crap" about gay marriage, for example, and said that anyone who did wasn't very smart.

Now, I probably won't be president or be of historical interest, just as his life won't be of interest to historians. But he made me feel as if there is something like a great American project. It included not just Lincoln, but every nineteenth-century self-made man. It includes not just FDR, but also my great-grandfather. And I imagine it's something I can continue through honest labor without making the history books.

THE CIRCLE OF LIFE

His Last Visit to Little Egypt

In 2007, Dad said he wanted to go back to southern Illinois to see his sister, Lura, who was ninety-seven at that time. Somehow I knew that he wanted to go alone with me. I first thought about flying, but since that would involve several plane changes, it seemed as if it would just be simpler for us to drive his Chrysler Sebring. I also felt in my heart that was what he wanted to do.

We started out on old Route 36, the same road that we had traveled when we brought him to live in Colorado. First, we visited his old stomping grounds in Springfield, Illinois. We were entertained by Lynn and Jeanne, children of his close friends who had passed away. While in Springfield, we took flowers to Mother's grave in Oak Ridge Cemetery. In two and a half years, Dad's ashes would be buried next to her there.

Over a couple of days, we took a combination of back roads and major expressways the almost two hundred miles south to Benton, Illinois, where my Aunt Lura was living with her daughter and son-in-law, Joy and Charlie Cash. Immediately upon arriving at their house in the country, Aunt Lura wanted us all to go out to lunch at the Maid Rite in nearby Zeigler. The little luncheonette only had counter seating. It was amazing to see the two over ninety-year-old siblings belly-up to the counter for one of their favorite treats.

Aunt Lura and Dad

The next day Joy drove Dad, Lura, and me around to old cemeteries in the area so we could look for family graves. In the first old cemetery, we located the joint headstone of Dad's siblings, Hallie (born in 1905 and died in 1906) and Emerson (born March 1912 and died May 1912). We also visited the cemetery where Aunt Rosie had been buried on a hilltop next to her husband, Frank. In West Frankfort, we observed the graves of Grandma and Grandpa Lee and several other family members at the Tower Heights Cemetery.

We also drove to the small hamlet of Akin and the surrounding, heavily wooded countryside between Akin and Macedonia where Dad was born. We saw Reed Ford Creek, Dad's old playing place, and the bridge near their old home, where a man named Eldon met my grandma. Although the house that Dad had been born in was gone, Uncle John's house was still there and occupied. It was difficult to believe that he, his wife, and their thirteen children had fit in this little house. The Baptist church where Dad's Grandpa Lee had sometimes preached was still there. Dad said he could visualize all of the horses and buggies surrounding the church on those long-ago Sunday mornings. That day we also drove by Aunt Rosie's farm and laughed at the memory of Dad's story about Till Bill, the bucking bull.

When we drove back to Colorado, I could tell that dad was contented with what would be his last visit to Little Egypt.

ACKNOWLEDGMENTS

In the preparation of this manuscript, my indebtedness is great to the following:

To my husband of fifty-five years, Bruce, who was supportive in many ways, including helping me navigate the process of submitting my manuscript to the online publisher. Further, for your constant belief that I could finish the three-year journey of writing this memoir about my wonderful father.

To Ann Gearing, my editor, who shared her notable talents and has earned my respect and admiration. I thank you for the time, energy, and patience you invested in developing this book.

To my son, Todd, who lovingly spoke of his grandfather's attributes at the Celebration of Life program and agreed to his eulogy being included in this memoir.

To my grandson, Isaiah, who expressed his memories of his great-grandfather and captured the essence of Dad's view of the changes that occurred during his long life.

To my cousin, Joy Cash, who cheerfully uncovered and shared many of our family photographs.

To my book club friend, Carolyn Brown, who provided resources and encouragement that spurred my efforts to get started writing Dad's story.